theatre & judaism

Theatre &
Series Editors: Jen Harvie and Dan Rebellato

theatre & judaism

Yair Lipshitz

methuen | drama

LONDON • NEW YORK • OXFORD • NEW DELHI • SYDNEY

METHUEN DRAMA
Bloomsbury Publishing Plc
50 Bedford Square, London, WC1B 3DP, UK
1385 Broadway, New York, NY 10018, USA
29 Earlsfort Terrace, Dublin 2, Ireland

BLOOMSBURY, METHUEN DRAMA and the Methuen Drama logo
are trademarks of Bloomsbury Publishing Plc

First published by RED GLOBE PRESS 2019
Reprinted by Methuen Drama 2022

A catalogue record for this book is available from the British Library.

A catalog record for this book is available from the Library of Congress.

ISBN: PB: 978-1-3520-0566-0
eBook: 978-1-3503-1626-3
ePDF: 978-1-3520-0567-7

Series: Theatre &

To find out more about our authors and books visit www.bloomsbury.com
and sign up for our newsletters.

contents

series editors' preface

The theatre is everywhere, from entertainment districts to the fringes, from the rituals of government to the ceremony of the courtroom, from the spectacle of the sporting arena to the theatres of war. Across these many forms stretches a theatrical continuum through which cultures both assert and question themselves.

Theatre has been around for thousands of years, and the ways we study it have changed decisively. It's no longer enough to limit our attention to the canon of Western dramatic literature. Theatre has taken its place within a broad spectrum of performance, connecting it with the wider forces of ritual and revolt that thread through so many spheres of human culture. In turn, this has helped make connections across disciplines; over the past fifty years, theatre and performance have been deployed as key metaphors and practices with which to rethink gender, economics, war, language, the fine arts, culture and one's sense of self.

Theatre & is a long series of short books which hopes to capture the restless interdisciplinary energy of theatre and performance. Each book explores connections between theatre and some aspect of the wider world, asking how the theatre might illuminate the world and how the world might illuminate the theatre. Each book is written by a leading theatre scholar and represents the cutting edge of critical thinking in the discipline.

We have been mindful, however, that the philosophical and theoretical complexity of much contemporary academic writing can act as a barrier to a wider readership. A key aim for these books is that they should all be readable in one sitting by anyone with a curiosity about the subject. The books are challenging, pugnacious, visionary sometimes and, above all, clear. We hope you enjoy them.

Jen Harvie and Dan Rebellato

theatre & judaism

Introduction: 'Totally Transformed'

Through several flashback sequences during the first season of Jill Soloway's web television series *Transparent* (2014), the viewers follow Ali Pfefferman (Emily Robinson), the youngest daughter of a mostly nonobservant Jewish-American family, as she is about to celebrate her Bat Mitzvah – the Jewish traditional coming-of-age rite of passage for girls. The seventh episode, 'The Symbolic Exemplar', shows Ali as she refuses to wear the dress purchased for the event, declares that she does not believe in God, and brings about the cancellation of the Bat Mitzvah. The eighth episode, 'Best New Girl', depicts the weekend when the Bat Mitzvah was supposed to take place, with Ali left alone at home. A bartender (Mel Shimkovitz), who was not notified of the cancellation, arrives. Ali admits to her that the alleged crisis of faith was in fact just an excuse to avoid the ceremony, since she was not sure she would be able to memorize the Torah reading. The Torah reading is the central part of the ritual in which the adolescent musically recites the weekly portion from the Pentateuch in the synagogue. Traditionally, and in most Jewish Orthodox communities today, only male adolescents perform the Torah reading. In liberal congregations, such as the one the Pfeffermans belong to, female adolescents perform it as well.

Immediately after her confession, however, Ali performs the Torah reading flawlessly in front of the bartender, who volunteers to be her 'captive audience'. Ali does not perform the Torah recital in the same manner she would have done in the synagogue. While correctly following the traditional ritual's text and the cantillation (the exact musicality of the text's chanting), Ali's choreography is far from traditional. As she stands up on the sofa and then hops onto the coffee table, Ali accompanies the recital with mock ballet moves and consciously overdramatic arm flailing, ending by diving with much flourish into a deep bow. To this, the bartender responds with: 'Oh my fucking God, that was brilliant. I have no idea what you just said but I feel totally transformed.'

In the synagogue, Ali's bodily movements would have been far more restrained. It is evident in the scene that teenage Ali enjoys presenting herself and her body to a slightly older young person. Ali's performance can therefore be seen as a theatricalization of the ritual, in the common meaning of 'theatricalization' as exaggerated self-display. Yet Ali also theatricalizes the ritual even more literally: she turns it into theatre, with the coffee table as stage and the bartender as audience. Her performance is theatrical also in the sense that she does not claim to conduct the 'real' ritual, but rather mimics it with much leeway for playfulness. Nevertheless, it does bring about a transformation in her audience – and arguably in her as well.

Being 'totally transformed' by this performance clearly resonates with the show's ongoing concern with transformations and transitions, which are at the core of *Transparent*, a series that follows the lives of Maura, a transgender woman, and her family. Transformations and transitions are also central to the specific verses from the Pentateuch that Ali recites as she performs her unexpected Torah reading. These are from Genesis 12:1–3:

> The Lord said to Abram, 'Go forth from your native land and from your father's house to the land that I will show you. I will make of you a great nation, and I will bless you; I will make your name great; and you shall be a blessing. I will bless those who bless you and curse him that curses you; and all the families on the earth shall bless themselves by you.'

Ali's transitions during her rite of passage, as well as Maura's journey towards realizing her identity as a transgender woman, both mirror the open-ended journey embarked upon by Abraham (then still called Abram). It is a journey to a promised yet unknown land. It requires leaving behind one's former identity so that one may become 'totally transformed'. By attaching the verses from Genesis to Ali's performance, the creators of *Transparent* studied the myth of Abraham's journey in terms of contemporary female puberty. They inquired in which ways the ancient religious text may illuminate a modern adolescent's journey, and how this adolescent body might unearth new meanings in the text through performance. Ali's re-enactment of the Bat Mitzvah ritual, the text she recites, and the context of the scene all interpret one another. As we will see later in this book, Ali participates, however nontraditionally, in a longer Jewish tradition that posits texts and their interpretations in the midst of religious performance.

But what about another transformation, that which takes place between religious ritual and theatricalized performance? What, if anything, is transformed there? Ali's impromptu performance of the Torah reading draws attention to the ways in which a specific individual body, with its particular concerns and anxieties, claims the scripted ritual as its own while performing outside the ritual context. At once freed from the demands of obligatory ritual and responsive to those demands on her own terms, Ali enters a multilayered bodily engagement with religious tradition – one that includes not just the text from Genesis, but also techniques of intonation and physical gestures. Theatricalization enables her to enter this engagement. It creates a playful space for her to reactivate the traditional ritual, perhaps more efficaciously than in the synagogue, in ways that are both distanced and dialogic.

This book explores the transformations that occur when Judaism meets theatre, especially concerning the three layers in Ali's scene: religious text, the traditional performance of it, and the theatrical performance of both. This is not a book about Jewish theatre, the boundaries of which are notoriously difficult to define. Rather, it is a book about the intersections and interventions between theatre and Jewish religious traditions. As we will see, theatre and Judaism are often conceived in terms of opposition and antagonism, but Ali's performance demonstrates how both transgressive and productive these relations can be. In what follows, I ask what happens when Jewish religious traditions are rethought through theatre, and vice versa.

I believe thinking about Jewish religious traditions along-side theatre is important these days because thinking about theatre and religion more broadly is important. Religion has resurfaced in recent years as a prominent factor in people's personal identities and in social and political debates worldwide. The 9/11 attacks and Western responses to them framed the political conflicts of the last two decades in religious terms. Immigration and growing multicultural-ism brought secular and religious communities into greater proximity with each other. Following the rise of identity politics, religious people call to consider religion an identity category that requires representation, like gender, sexual-ity, or ethnicity. Religions worldwide, including Judaism, figure predominantly in the public sphere in ways that they did not a few decades ago. Consider, for example, current disputes in the USA as to whether declining to cater gay weddings is within one's religious freedoms, or debates in France regarding the wearing of hijabs by Muslim female students in the public school system. Philosopher Jürgen Habermas (2006, 2008) consequently suggested that we now live in 'post-secular' societies, that their secularity can no longer be taken for granted, and that the role of religion in civil society needs to be negotiated anew.

This short book is composed of two parts. The first (the next two sections) is historiographical in nature, and critically tackles how narratives about theatre in Jewish societies often address religion and secularity. The second part, the remainder of the book, offers an alternative to the common narrative. Rather than thinking about theatre in terms of secularization, I propose to consider it as a form of study, an embodied exegesis. These are concepts I borrow from Jewish religious traditions, but that also allow critical distance from these very same traditions. Like Ali's performance, I will argue, theatre may offer a playful mechanism for engaging with and reinterpreting the presence of religion in contemporary society. I propose that through performance, theatre may register both ruptures and continuities with religious traditions, and thus enable a shared inquiry for society into the place of religion and secularity nowadays.

Part I

'Tradition, tradition!': Religion, Secularization, and Theatre

To begin, the relations between Judaism, religion, and theatre need clarification. The term 'Judaism' is difficult to define. In contemporary culture, one may use the adjective 'Jewish' to refer to religion (as in 'Jewish faith'), to ethnicity (as in 'Jewish-American'), to culture ('Jewish humor'), or to nationality (in the case of Israel as a 'Jewish state'). In today's world, these usages do not always coincide. One can identify ethnically as Jewish but have nothing to do with Jewish religious practices or beliefs. This has led to the modern occasional differentiation between *Jewishness* as ethnic identity and *Judaism* as religion. Historically, however, these aspects were intermingled. Simply put, up until the nineteenth century, a Jewish person was both part of an ethnic group and an observant of a religion at the same time, in ways that made it almost meaningless to differentiate between the two. This book will not center on the ethnic component of Jewish identity and its manifestations in the theatre, in works by Jewish and non-Jewish artists alike, mainly because that area has already received great attention in scholarship (the reader is encouraged to consult the 'Further Reading' section at the end of the book for references). Judaism as religious tradition, on the other hand, has not yet been treated as extensively in relation to theatre.

Even applying the term 'religious' to those strands of Jewish culture I will highlight here is hardly simple. We should recall that for centuries people did not describe themselves as 'religious', or what they did or believe in as 'religion'.

The category of religion, as a seemingly overarching and universal category that embraces a variety of practices and beliefs in different societies, only began to emerge in Europe in the sixteenth and seventeenth centuries. According to Talal Asad (1993) and Jonathan Z. Smith (1998), this happened following internal political developments within European Christianity, and due to the encounter of Europeans with other cultures through exploration, trade, and colonization. This would mean that the concept of 'religion' – not the practices and beliefs themselves, but as a category for the understanding of culture and self – is relatively recent and was coined in European and Christian terms to be applied to other societies. In a book from 2011, *How Judaism Became a Religion*, Leora Batnitzky argues that the very understanding of Judaism *as* a religion is also a modern phenomenon. According to Batnitzky, during the late eighteenth and nineteenth centuries, recently emancipated European Jews attempted to integrate into their surrounding societies and had to define who they were in the wider European (mainly Protestant) terms of what religion was – or to find other, nonreligious forms of self-definition. Such developments radically altered the self-understanding of Jews and the way others perceived them, segregating some elements in Jewish culture from others, dubbing some 'religious' and others as not.

When I speak of Jewish 'religious' traditions I therefore do so for the sake of convenience, while being aware that I am anachronistically applying a modern category on texts and practices that are of mainly premodern origins. I will use the term 'religious' to describe texts that Jews have seen as either given by God in the Hebrew Bible or as authoritative interpretations of those texts, and practices considered by Jewish communities to fulfill God's commandments. This is hardly an exhaustive definition, but it will suffice for our purposes here.

When considered as a religion, Judaism is hardly monolithic. Seeing itself rooted in the Hebrew Bible (also commonly known as the Old Testament), each period of Jewish religious history reinterpreted, and at times radically remolded, its predecessors, turning Judaism into a richly multilayered religious heritage. Even within each period, contesting sects, movements, or denominations fiercely debated Judaism's fundamental precepts. What one Jewish community may consider foundational for Judaism others will regard as secondary or even negligible. Rather than assuming any inherently Jewish religious worldview, I therefore speak of Jewish religious traditions in the plural, to suggest networks of intertwining and diverging actions, concepts, and texts that cumulate in the many ways Judaism has been, and is, practiced and experienced as a religion.

Theatre's relation to religion is of course nothing new. One of the most prominent narratives in theatre historiography had been the emergence of Western theatre out of religious ritual. In 1912, Jane Harrison and Gilbert Murray, members of the Cambridge School of Anthropology, presented in the book *Themis* the thesis that delineates the growth of Greek tragedy from ancient rites. In his 1903 book *The Mediaeval Stage*, E.K. Chambers was among several scholars who proposed a similar evolutionary development in the Middle Ages, as Christian liturgical drama gradually moved outside of the Church and became secularized, in the sense that plays were no longer produced by the clergy. Note that such a narrative puts religion and theatre in a linear sequence in time: the latter develops from the former, breaks free from it as it were. Theatre leaves religious ritual in the past even as it retains some of ritual's elements, in order to become an autonomous artistic endeavor. This narrative held sway in theatre historiography for quite a while, even though scholars continuously criticized its evolutionary model and scrutinized many of its various elements. It was still prevalent enough in 1996 for theatre historian Thomas Postlewait to caution against the 'assumed binarism' between 'religion and theatre, ritual and play [...] the primordial and the modern' that is at risk of falsifying the theatre 'history we write and teach' (p. 2).

This narrative is in fact part of a broader scholarly discussion about religion and secularization in Western societies. During most of the twentieth century, the idea that religion is in constant decline in Western society (and some would argue, globally) has governed much of social theory. This idea is often referred to as the 'secularization thesis' or 'secularization theory'. The term 'secularization' can mean a great many things, and may occur on various levels of personal and social life, such as individual faith, observance of ritual practices, or Church membership. For the current discussion, I will focus on two aspects of secularization: the *societal* differentiation between the public and private spheres, and the *temporal* framing of secularization as a movement from the past to the modern present.

Let us begin with the societal dimension. Sociologist Bryan Wilson (1976) influentially argued that while on a personal level, contemporary people might still have faith in God or participate in ritual, they nevertheless do so in a modern society with an inherently secular *structure*. By this, Wilson means that religion ceased to hold significant power in the public sphere of politics, law, and economics. The modern public sphere is considered to be devoid of religious concerns and practices, and governed by rational, empirical, secular standards and procedures. In this secular structure of modern society, religion is relegated to the private sphere, to the individual choices of people who may or may not be religious.

However, as mentioned earlier, recent decades have witnessed the return of religion to the public sphere and the political arena. This development brought about a wave of critique against the secularization theory. Already in a 1994 book, *Public Religions in the Modern World*, José Casanova challenged the notion that in modern times religion is consigned to the private sphere, and noted the public role it still often plays in many societies worldwide. Since the publication of that book, religion has gained even more decisive impact in the public sphere, thus casting serious doubt on Wilson's definition of secularization. For our purposes, if the post-secular moment is marked by the return of religion to the public sphere, then theatre can prove an extremely rich site through which to probe these dynamics.

Christopher Balme, in *The Theatrical Public Sphere* (2014), highlights theatre's potential to participate in the public sphere. Theatre is a social practice of shared, common intellectual as well as physical space for debating and negotiating society's conflicts and underlying tensions. As such, it holds much value as a site for examining religion's place in the public sphere today.

The concept of secularization relegates religion not only to the private sphere but also to the past, which leads us to the temporal dimension. Secularization theory considered the decline of religion to be fundamental to modernization, and it portrayed a picture of linear progress in which religion is associated with the past. This is already rooted in the Enlightenment worldview of the eighteenth century, and its perception of the history of humankind as a story of progress towards rationality and maturation (with secularity equated with both). In the late nineteenth century, Edward B. Tylor, one of the founders of the anthropological study of religion, formulated a model of cultural evolution in which early forms of religion (considered at the time as 'primitive' or 'savage') gave way to more sophisticated forms, and finally to rational scientific knowledge. The idea of cultural evolution has since then fallen out of grace in academia. Its effects, however, still reverberate in the social studies and the humanities through the notion that religion somehow points backwards and secularity forward. In his 1976 essay, for example, Bryan Wilson wrote that in the modern world 'religion is a remnant' (p. 266) – a thing of the past. This results, as Ann Pellegrini and Janet R. Jakobsen observe in their introduction to *Secularisms* (2008), in the common yet striking attitude 'that some societies are "stuck in time" or "caught in a different century" despite the fact that they exist contemporaneously with societies understood to be more modern' (pp. 5–6).

However, religion nowadays appears as modern a phenomenon as secularism. With the resurgence of religion at the end of the twentieth century, scholars called to reevaluate the secularization theory's notion of temporal progress. Peter Berger, a noted sociologist of religion who promoted the secularization theory in his earlier work, announced the 'desecularization' of the world in a 1999 book and claimed that the secularization theory was misguided. For other critics, the question was not whether religion 'returned', but rather whether it ever left to begin with. In a 1999 paper, 'Secularization R.I.P.', Rodney Stark claimed that historians and sociologists overstated both the religiosity of the past and the secularity of the present, thus creating a deeper sense of rupture than was indeed the case and accentuating the image of historical progress from religion to secularity. Talal Asad and others criticized the thesis also from a postcolonial viewpoint, arguing that it conflates secularization with modernization, and interprets other cultures and traditions through Western-Christian categories that do not take into account the differing interplays between religion, secularity, and modernity in non-Western and non-Christian cultures. All these critics share an attempt to unsettle what they see as secularization theory's unilinear and universal trajectory of history from religious past to secular present.

Not all scholars agree that the notion of secularization needs to be entirely discarded. A few, like Steve Bruce, staunchly defend the secularization thesis as is, but others maintain that it merits a more nuanced consideration – one that does not presume the inevitable, all-encompassing, and global triumph of secularism. Philosopher Charles Taylor, for example, in his 2007 book *A Secular Age*, argues that the modern period can be still seen as secular because the conditions of religious belief have changed. In the past, claims Taylor, not believing in God was not a viable option, but today it is. Religion did not disappear, yet it became a matter of personal choice. Religions contend against other religions, and especially against the possibility of not being religious at all. Being religious is one option among many in a global marketplace of ideas and identities. Note that such a line of thought does not relegate religion to the past, or to the private sphere, but also does not deny the emergence of the secular, especially as an identity category. It allows us to think of religiosity and secularity as contemporaneous and consider the myriad ways in which they coexist, intersect, and interact. This of course entails a different approach to the topic of theatre and religion than the historical narrative according to which secular theatre supplanted religious ritual. Instead, a model of simultaneous interactions between religion, secularity, and theatre may prove to be more fruitful.

To begin with, religion does not always play a conservative or 'backwards' role in society or in the theatre. It does not always pull towards the past. Osip Dymov's Yiddish play *Bronx Express*

(New Jewish Theatre, New York, 1919) can help illuminate this point. The play follows Khatskl (later Harry) Hungerproud, a poor Jewish immigrant in New York who, while priding himself on being Socialist, also yearns to make it big in America. In a dream sequence that is the bulk of the play, Khatskl strikes a deal with the millionaires of corporate America and advises them to tempt their Jewish employees into working on Yom Kippur, the holiest fast day in the Jewish religious calendar, by offering them double or triple payment. By luring them away from their religious cultural identities and 'Americanizing' them, their employers will be able to subjugate the Jews fully to the workplace. In Khatskl's vision, this will bring about an America with 'No holidays, no religion, no tradition [...] Everyone cooked in the same pot' (p. 295). The image of America as melting pot becomes a dystopia, where all cultures lose their particularity and become part of a machine that 'works and buys, works and buys' (ibid.), serving an industrial-consumerist system. When later in the play a friend of Khatskl reports that the Jews have indeed forsaken Yom Kippur for the sake of better wages, Khatskl shrugs: 'a man must eat, after all'. To this, his friend replies: 'A man must fast' (p. 301). Spiritual needs are no less vital to a person's, or a community's, survival than the physical ones, the play seems to argue. The capitalist economic system maybe attends to the latter, but deprives one of the former. In *Bronx Express*, then, religion aligns with a leftist worldview, and enables a radical, rather than conservative, critique of Capitalism. In its name, Dymov also expresses a surprisingly early multicultural sensitivity to the perils of an immigrant society under economic duress. The language of religious tradition serves Dymov to empower a critical oppositional stance in present-day social struggles – not as a voice of the past, but as a vehicle for paving a way to a better future.

Yet theatre unsettles the relegation of religion to the past not only explicitly through a specific play's content. By its very mechanism, theatre deeply complicates attempts to delineate any simple, straightforward trajectory from (religious) past to (secular) present. Time in the theatre, in the words of Rebecca Schneider in her contribution to this series (2014), is 'decidedly porous and pockmarked with other times' (p. 7). Theatre is an art of the present, but often represents, cites, and echoes the past. It happens in the 'here and now' but is also repetitive and involves rehearsals. Linear, cyclical, and ephemeral experiences of time all coalesce in the theatrical event. In a 2010 essay, theatre scholar Tracy C. Davis coined the term 'performative time' to describe a nonlinear temporality that overturns 'a straightforward concept of temporal succession' (p. 149). In performance, the past becomes present. It reverberates in the here and now rather than being left behind.

If theatrical performance has the capacity to dismantle the notion of temporal succession – of the past giving way to the present – then it can likewise unsettle the idea of secularity straightforwardly succeeding religion, even in cases when on the surface it does not aim to do so. This can be seen in what is perhaps the most globally widespread modern theatrical representation of Judaism: *Fiddler on the*

Roof (book by Joseph Stein; Broadway premiere: Imperial Theatre, New York, 1964). This musical famously has as its opening number the song 'Tradition' (lyrics: Sheldon Harnick; music: Jerry Bock), a spectacular tour de force celebrating the traditional religious Jewish community in an Eastern European village at the turn of the century. In this community, 'tradition' is connected to patriarchal gender and family roles, to religious observance that expresses devotion to God, and to a clear idea of each person as to what God expects them to do.

'Tradition' is an electrifyingly catchy opening sequence, declaring the vitality of religious tradition for Jewish survival. However, precisely its position as an *opening* sequence places it as a relic of the past that the protagonist, Tevye, and the community, must leave behind as the plot progresses. In *Fiddler*, Tevye struggles with his daughters' nontraditional choices of marriage. The first marries for love rather than through an organized match with a wealthier, older man. The second falls in love with a Socialist idealist. The third converts to Christianity in order to marry her non-Jewish lover. Tevye learns to loosen his concept of tradition for the sake of his daughters' happiness (which he manages with the first two daughters, but hardly with the third).

By the end of the musical, following the Russian government's decree expelling all Jews from the village, Tevye's family plans to leave for America. This is a stark deviation from the musical's source, Sholem Aleichem's prose narrative *Tevye the Dairyman* that was published serially between 1895 and 1914. While *Tevye the Dairyman* ends with a far more ambiguous tone regarding Tevye's final destination, *Fiddler on the Roof*'s trajectory is clear: from 'Tradition' to liberal America, leaving the former, however painfully, in the past. Tevye may remain traditionally religious but his descendants in America – like those watching the musical in the auditorium – will presumably be less so. *Fiddler* treats religious tradition with loving affection and nostalgia, but it also portrays it as a world clearly left behind. While not straightforwardly showing secularity onstage, the musical seems to participate in some popular version of the secularization narrative.

Indeed, this temporal narrative is implied in the very term 'tradition'. As Hizky Shoham (2011) observes, 'tradition' has often come to signify a stagnant, past-oriented society, as opposed to the dynamism of modernity (p. 317). In this sense, like religion, tradition serves as the other of modernity – relegated to the past, or to 'traditional societies' that allegedly still live in the past. By beginning the musical in announcing, however buoyantly, their commitment to tradition, Tevye's community situate itself in bygone times. However, Shoham continues to suggest another definition of tradition. Rather than considering traditions as activities or beliefs that hail from the past, Shoham proposes to consider tradition as a practice in the present of assigning temporal meaning to these activities or beliefs. Traditions do not simply exist as a given within a specific culture, but are granted the status of 'traditional' by communities and individuals. Through referring to practices and concepts as 'traditions', society registers continuities as well as changes between past, present, and future (p. 315). Traditionality is therefore performative, constructed in the present in order to relate to the past. In other words, by labeling Jewish religious life 'Tradition', *Fiddler on the Roof* does not describe but *constructs* it as such. The musical might relegate religious tradition to the past, but it does so in the present time of performance.

Furthermore, it does so again and again, night after night. *Fiddler on the Roof*, like most other musicals, is itself performed according to its own traditions such as score, choreography, orchestration, set design, and costumes. All of these are often kept quite meticulously and even reverently. Audiences who attend *Fiddler* usually come to see something familiar occur once more. Rather than depicting a narrative of progress, *Fiddler on the Roof* in fact performs this narrative repeatedly. The cyclical repetitiveness of performance runs counter to the linear trajectory of the plot. On one level, *Fiddler on the Roof* seems to advocate the secularization thesis, by situating religious traditions in the past. On another level, ironically, it serves as a ritual for a modern secular society, as it repeatedly conjures the very same past it allegedly leaves behind. If secularization is seen as a way of affixing a differentiation between the past and the present, and delineating a progressive process from one to the other, then theatre challenges and complicates the temporal imagination of the secularization thesis. Theatre creates entanglements of linearity and repetitiveness, of performance's present time and the pasts it conjures, even when, as in *Fiddler*, it seemingly seeks to affirm ideas of progress and secularization.

This is one of my reasons for emphasizing earlier that in discussing theatre and Judaism I wish to consider simultaneous interactions rather than narratives of progression and succession. As we will now see in detail, much of the discussion of theatre and Jewish religion has been often framed in terms of secularization, with modern secular theatre succeeding Jewish religious tradition. I believe this model is unhelpful in many ways, especially because it relegates Judaism (and other religions) to an unenlightened past. In what follows, I will outline the dominant narratives that posit Jewish religion and theatre in terms of opposition to each other, and explain why I find these narratives unsatisfactory. The rest of the book will be devoted to offering an alternative.

Narratives of Opposition and Secularization

The idea that theatre emerged in Jewish societies due to their secularization became prevalent in theatre historiography for two main reasons: the relative lack of theatrical activity in Jewish societies prior to the late nineteenth century, and several texts by Jewish religious authorities that responded to theatre with clear hostility. These gave rise to a view commonly held by theatre scholars and practitioners alike that Jewish religion is somehow inherently opposed to theatre, and that theatre could thrive in Jewish societies only once they broke away from the constraints of religion and became secular.

Unlike the societies surrounding them, Jews were seldom involved in theatrical activity up until the late nineteenth century. At least according to the evidence we have, there was apparently no continuous dramatic or theatrical tradition that will enable speaking of 'Jewish theatre' as a clearly defined practice. Whenever theatre or drama did emerge in Jewish societies, they did so through various intercultural encounters with (mainly) Western theatre. However, in many cases, Jewish religious authorities responded to these encounters with suspicion.

The most notable and influential religious response was that of the Rabbis to the arrival of ancient Roman theatre to Palestine. The Rabbis (also sometimes referred to as the Sages) were a group of Jewish scholars that were active in Palestine and Babylonia during the first centuries CE. Their output was an enormous assemblage of legal and exegetical writings that reinterpreted the biblical verses and formed Jewish religion anew. These interpretations and the debates surrounding them were gathered in compilations known collectively as 'rabbinic literature', including the Mishnah (redacted c. 200 CE), the Palestinian and Babylonian Talmuds (the former assumed to have been compiled around 400 CE; the latter around 600 CE), and other works. All of these eventually became the cornerstone of Jewish curricula of religious studies for centuries.

As part of the expansion of the Roman Empire and its culture, theatre arrived in Palestine as well. At the time, it was mainly composed of gladiatorial matches, theatricalized executions, and sexually explicit comic mimes and pantomimes. Like several Church Fathers at roughly the same time, such as Tertullian (c. 160–c. 225) and St. John Chrysostom (c. 349–407), the Rabbis responded to the theatre with downright animosity. Rabbinic literature regularly

contrasted going to the theatre with Jewish religious observance, such as prayer, and the study of the Torah (the Jewish
law derived from the Hebrew Bible, or more broadly, the
entirety of Jewish religious knowledge). Aside from very few
circumstances in which it was permitted, the Rabbis prohib-
ited going to the Roman theatre, reasoning that it involved
pagan idolatry, that the spectators were complicit with the
murderous acts occurring onstage, or simply that it was a
frivolous activity and a waste of time that could be used for
religious matters. Beyond that, the Rabbis saw the theatre as
a representation of the culture of the other: Roman culture
at a time of imperialism and colonization.

A prayer composed by the Rabbis, which appears in the
Palestinian Talmud, demonstrates their overall attitude to
the theatre. A scholar is to recite this prayer once he (scholars were only male at the time) leaves the *beit-midrash*, the
hall of study:

> I am grateful before you, Lord, my God and the
> God of my ancestors, that you gave me a portion
> among those who dwell in the *beit-midrash* and the
> synagogue, and not [among those who dwell] in
> the theatres and the circuses. For I labor and they
> labor; I am diligent, and they are diligent. I labor
> to inherit the Garden of Eden, and they labor to
> reach the nethermost Pit [Tractate *Berachot* 4:2].

The prayer portrays mirror institutions that display similar
traits yet are diametrically opposed, with each pair identified

with a different social group. The text presents the *beit-midrash*, the theatre, the synagogue, and the circus as establishments where labor takes place, and we might add that they are all spaces of performance – be that entertainment, liturgy, or scholarly performance. This analogy, however, serves the Rabbis only to put the opposition into sharper relief, and entirely divorce the theatre from the synagogue and the *beit-midrash*. This does not mean that Jewish people at the time of the Rabbis did not frequent the theatre alongside the synagogue and participate in the activities of both. As Zeev Weiss demonstrates in his book *Public Spectacles in Roman and Late Antique Palestine* (2014), Roman entertainment culture deeply permeated Jewish society in Late Ancient Palestine, including rabbinic circles. In a sense, the prayer probably tries to rectify precisely such a situation, and instill in the praying person's consciousness a clear-cut distinction while reality was far more muddled.

Perhaps because of the defining influence of the Rabbis on the subsequent development of Jewish religion, or for other reasons, there is very little evidence of theatrical activities by Jews in Europe from the Middle Ages until modern times, with a few notable exceptions, even while such activity flourished among their Christian neighbors. There is even less evidence of theatre in Jewish communities in Muslim countries. Other forms of performance and entertainment did exist in Jewish communities, such as folk plays and wedding jesters, but the establishment of theatre as we know it from Western culture was mainly absent. The beginning of a continuous theatrical activity within

Jewish society up until today dates as late as the 1870s, and stems from the efforts of Avrom Goldfaden (1840–1908), a prolific playwright and founder of the first professional Yiddish troupe in Iași, Romania. Yiddish was the common vernacular spoken by Jews of (mainly Eastern) European origin for centuries, while Hebrew was mostly reserved for liturgy and other sacred practices, and was not spoken on a daily basis. Yiddish was therefore the language that Goldfaden's newly trained actors could easily speak onstage, and his audiences could understand. Only several decades later would Hebrew resume its role as a spoken everyday language, including in the theatre.

Goldfaden was active at a time of much turmoil in European Jewish society, which was undergoing processes of urbanization, modernization, mass immigration, and in some cases secularization as well. He was part of an intellectual movement known as the *haskalah* (often referred to as the Jewish Enlightenment, but more accurately translated as 'the acquisition of knowledge'), a movement that called for the greater integration of Jews in modern European cultural and intellectual life. Wishing to acquaint Jewish audiences with European culture, and specifically with theatre, Goldfaden wed the agenda of the *haskalah* with forms of popular entertainment, in order to develop a theatrical language that was enthusiastically received by Yiddish-speaking audiences. After this turning point, theatre flourished in Jewish societies, also in other languages and worldwide.

In the twentieth century, when scholars wished to explain the relative lack of Jewish theatrical activity prior to the late nineteenth century, they often resorted to the rabbinic hostile response to Roman theatre in Late Antiquity and saw it as indicative of an inherent opposition to theatre, deeply imbued in Judaism's religious mind-set. Philosopher Martin Buber (1878–1965), for example, is one of many to maintain that monotheistic Judaism, in which there is only one final truth-claim – that of God – cannot accommodate drama's multiplicity of conflicting truths. 'Agamemnon, Clytemnestra, Orestes are both right and wrong,' writes Buber in 1929, but the Jews understand 'that there is a being right, a rightness, one who is right – that God is right' (pp. 89–90). From a different angle, theatre scholar Shimon Levy, who describes Jewish religion as 'theatrophobic' in his introduction to *Theatre and Holy Script* (1999), proposes that Judaism rejected theatre because it was threatened by its performative power 'to transform matter into spirit and vice versa', which in traditional Judaism should be 'the exclusive prerogative of God' (pp. 2–3).

The main problem with these lines of argument is that not one single Jewish religious text ever gives any of these reasons to reject theatre. These are modern conceptualizations regarding what both theatre and Judaism are, projected backwards. It is true that rabbinic literature speaks against attending 'theatres' in general, which perhaps propelled later Jews in other times and places who follow rabbinic ordinance to continue abstaining from the theatre. The Rabbis, however, denounced a particular kind of theatre in a specific set of historical circumstances, not theatre as some kind of universal category. They articulated their reasons explicitly:

idolatry, bloodshed, overall immorality, and waste of time. The Rabbis considered Roman theatre to be a sinful place, to be sure, but nowhere do they theorize about theatricality being theologically dangerous as such. This is not to say that the Rabbis would have become theatre enthusiasts if they had encountered *Antigone* rather than bloody Roman spectacles, but it is to say that it is impossible to infer some inherent, essential opposition between theatre and Jewish religion out of particular historical contingencies.

Another version of the oppositional scheme serves also to explain theatre's emergence in modern Jewish society as a token of secularization. If theatre and Jewish religion are set in intrinsic antagonism, it stands to reason that theatre could only grow in Jewish societies once they left the constraints of religion behind. These accounts portray a historiographical narrative in which, after years of religious repression, theatre finally prevailed. Eli Rozik's *Jewish Drama & Theatre: From Rabbinical Intolerance to Secular Liberalism* (2013) can serve as a relatively recent example. The very title of the book is revealing, as it charts a dichotomous binary between a religious, anti-theatrical past, and a secular, theatrical present. It also delineates an emancipatory trajectory from the one to the other, equating the former with intolerance and the latter with liberalism. Rozik ends his book by explicating this trajectory:

> The neutral nature of the theatre medium as an instrument of thinking and communicating thinking, i.e., in being able to formulate and communicate even contradicting thoughts, was

probably perceived by the Jewish religious establishment as a threat, leading to the conclusions that only a secular and liberal society can bring about the full realization of theatre's potentialities (p. 297).

For Rozik, religiosity and secularity comprise entirely opposite modes of being and thinking – with theatre deeply allied with the latter. This account raises many questions, not least because theatre flourished in the West exactly in its capacity to 'formulate and communicate even contradicting thoughts' in societies that were markedly unsecular, such as Classical Athens or Elizabethan England. Furthermore, perceiving any religion as threatened by thinking, and as incapable of communicating contradictory thoughts, is an extremely reductive view, and it is simply baffling in the current context. After all, the Talmud – where many of the Jewish religious establishment's objections to the theatre are registered – famously, almost stereotypically, thrives precisely on thinking and communicating contradicting thoughts. Rozik therefore channels the historiography of theatre in Jewish culture through his own value judgment of religion and secularism.

It is undeniable that theatre appeared in modern Jewish society at a moment when there was a sea change in its history, in which many Jews attempted to integrate into their surrounding societies – and in some cases (but definitely not all) consequently reconsidered their religious obligations or abandoned them altogether. It is also true that, as far as we know, those who produced theatre in Jewish societies in Europe, the Americas, and Palestine in the late nineteenth and early twentieth centuries were mostly Jews who would probably be considered secular, or at least certainly non-Orthodox. Yet while there are evident links between theatre and processes of secularization in Jewish modernity, one should be wary of drawing too firm a line between past and present, between religion and secularity, which might misrepresent both.

The (admittedly few) cases of Jewish theatrical activity prior to the period in which secularization supposedly occurred, can serve to illuminate this point. One remarkable such case took place in early modern Italy. During the sixteenth century, at the same time as Christian scholars, playwrights, and actors all over Italy experimented with revisiting and reviving classical comedies, tragedies, and theatrical venues, Jewish communities and individuals participated in this endeavor in various ways. Most famous of these is Leone de' Sommi (or Yehudah Sommo, as was his Hebrew name), a prolific playwright, set designer, choreographer, and the author of an innovative theoretical treatise on theatre production in Italian. He was the head of the Jewish theatre troupe in Mantua, who staged Italian plays at the Gonzaga ducal court for most of the sixteenth century. Leone de' Sommi is also probably the author of the earliest known play written in Hebrew: *A Comedy of Betrothal* (Mantua, c. 1550). This play, written in the genre of Italian Renaissance comedy, but with Jewish characters and concerns, is a bold and innovative attempt in writing comedy in a language considered a holy tongue at the time. Writing a comedy in Hebrew might therefore seem to modern readers as a secularization of the language, but de' Sommi and the Jewish community of Mantua were of course not 'secular' in any way. In modern terms they would have been considered 'religious' Jews, although if we recall Batnitzky's argument that Judaism was reconceived as a religion only centuries later, clearly this adjective would have been meaningless for a sixteenth-century person. The Jews of Mantua were neither religious nor secular, because these definitions did not exist, but they observed Jewish law like all other communities at the time. We have evidence of the Jewish troupe in Mantua requesting not to perform in court during the Sabbath or in Jewish holidays, so that they would not violate the religious laws of these days. Leone de' Sommi himself founded a synagogue in Mantua. There is no indication whatsoever that the Mantuan Jews saw any contradiction between their theatrical activity and their religious observance. For them, being theatrically active clearly did not have any secularizing effect. The notion of theatre as a product of secularization is simply inadequate for explaining the Jewish-Mantuan community – religiously observant and theatrically active at the same time.

Once we reach modernity, theatre at times did take a part in the culture wars that raged in the nineteenth and twentieth centuries between secular and religious Jews, and often staunchly sided with the secular camp by staging harsh critique and scathing parodies of traditional religion. As we have seen in the case of *Bronx Express*, however, in other instances plays took positions that are far more complex. Yet even beyond the content of this play or that, the very practice of making theatre in modern Jewish societies often unsettled any clear-cut divisions between the religious and the secular. The success of Goldfaden, 'the father of modern Jewish theatre', can be attributed in many ways precisely to his ability to incorporate elements from Jewish religious traditions into his modern theatre, in a manner that appealed to wide audiences. In an essay from 1899, for example, Goldfaden reflects on his practice of borrowing music for his plays from the liturgical melodies used by cantors in the synagogue. He portrays a picture in which 'it often occurred that a melody was sung in the synagogue and used for dances on my stage at the same time in the very same town' (p. 256). This is hardly an image of theatre supplanting the synagogue, but rather of both establishments existing side by side in ongoing conversation.

And finally, the scope of the discussion regarding the secularity of theatre in modern Jewish cultures has to be broadened both historically and geographically. The rise of secularism in the nineteenth and twentieth centuries was of course not the culmination of Jewish history, and many Jews today continue intermixing religion and secularity in various forms, and shaping new constellations and identities, including in the theatre. In Israel, for example, recent years have shown a considerable growth of theatrical activity among Orthodox Jews, who bring their own religious concerns to the stage. Geographically, the predominantly European discourse outlined above is not easily applicable to Jews in Muslim countries (and later Mizrahi Jews around the globe), who responded to modernity on their own terms, which often did not embrace the religious/secular dichotomy to begin with. One needs to approach the theatre produced in these contexts with more flexible, or entirely different, paradigms regarding the relations between religion, secularity, and theatre.

To conclude, without underestimating the enormous crises, ruptures, and revolutions experienced by Jewish societies and individuals in modernity with regard to religion, seeing theatre merely as a token of a straightforward secularization process runs the risk of obscuring continuities and participations in the interrelations between theatre and Jewish religious traditions. Most importantly, it may draw our attention away from the ways in which theatre and Jewish religious traditions illuminate each other even in modern times. I now move to explore some of these mutual illuminations.

Part II

'And Now We Will Perform an Exegesis'

Any account of Jewish religious traditions will have to rec-
ognize the centrality of texts and textual activities to many
of them. In *People of the Book: Canon, Meaning, and Authority*
(1997), philosopher Moshe Halbertal maintains:

> In the Jewish tradition the centrality of the text
> takes the place of theological consistency. Jews
> have had diverse and often opposing ideas about
> God [...] These conceptions of God have little
> in common and they are specifically Jewish only
> insofar as each is a genuine interpretation of a
> Jewish canonical text.
>
> Not only does the text provide a common
> background for various ideas and practices, but
> also text-centeredness itself has deeper implica-
> tions. Some of the major developments in Jewish
> tradition can be understood through the commu-
> nity's notions of its relation to text, of what text
> is, and how text functions in its midst. Text is
> thus more than a shared matrix for a diverse tra-
> dition – it is one of the tradition's central opera-
> tive concepts, like 'God' or 'Israel' (pp. 1–2).

While I am wary of speaking about '*the* Jewish tradition', I
do find Halbertal's account to be an extremely compelling
portrayal of most Jewish religious cultures. In these cultures, texts are not just a medium for some abstract, purely
mental activity. They are deeply integrated in embodied

performance. In religious ritual, texts are vocally recited, like the Torah reading in the synagogue that Ali re-enacted in *Transparent*. They also serve as material objects to be worn over the body (inside the *tefillin*, or phylacteries – small black leather boxes containing parchments with biblical verses, that are put on the forehead and the upper arm during prayer) and placed in space (inside the *mezuzah*, a small case containing biblical verses and located at doorposts). In all these cases, text is an ingredient within the live material event of ritual performance. As we have noticed in the scene from *Transparent*, texts and performances also often maintain reciprocal interpretive relations in Jewish religious practices that theatre can also reactivate.

In *Notes on Akiba* (The Jewish Museum, New York, 1995), a short play by Jewish-American playwright Tony Kushner, the playwright and his friend Michael Mayer portray each other as they prepare *charoset*, a traditional food for the ritual of the Pesach Seder. Pesach, or Passover, is a Jewish springtime weeklong holiday that celebrates the Exodus of the Israelites from slavery in Egypt. The Seder is an annual nightly ritual, taking place during the first evening of Pesach, and consisting mainly of a long meal that includes various symbolic foods and the recital of the *haggadah*, a text through which the story of the Exodus is retold.

Notes on Akiba begins by presenting the play: 'These are notes on Akiba. This is exegesis, or elaboration' (p. 245). 'Exegesis' comes from the Greek, 'to lead out', and its etymology implies that the text harbors a meaning that is not directly communicated, and therefore needs to be actively extracted through hermeneutic techniques. Later, the term has come to be mainly associated with the interpretation of religious Scripture. The notion of 'elaboration' is later referred to directly by the performers:

MICHAEL: [...] The more one elaborates.
TONY: Elaborates. E-LAB-OR-ATES. *Elaborates*.
MICHAEL: On the departure from Egypt the more praiseworthy one is. (pp. 246–47; original emphasis)

This is a statement taken from the *haggadah*, although a more literal translation of the Hebrew original would be: 'the more one tells the story of the departure from Egypt, the more praiseworthy it is.' While the *haggadah* prescribes to tell the story of the Exodus, it peculiarly does not provide an extended narrative of the event. Rather, it is comprised of a series of rabbinic exegeses (or *midrashim*) elaborating on several verses that relate the event. The Seder, in this sense, is a performative ritual that relives the Exodus through textual interpretation rather than storytelling. More precisely, it considers exegesis, or elaboration, *as* a form of storytelling. Kushner follows this correlation in his play.

While the notion of exegesis is commonly linked mainly to textual interpretation, Kushner elaborates not so much about the story of the Exodus but rather about the Seder ritual itself. He and Mayer interpret the symbolic foods and various local customs, discuss at length his father's propensity to skip the boring parts of the *haggadah*, and finally offer their own exegesis on one of those parts everyone skips. Even the skipping itself, this seeming lack of reverence to ritual tradition, receives exegetical attention: 'And now we will perform an exegesis on the traditional lack of exegesis concerning this passage' (p. 255). In short, Kushner's performance is an exegesis on the performance of the Seder, and not just on the text. *Notes on Akiba* thus exemplifies how texts are entangled in Jewish religious traditions with a variety of embodied practices. Food, biblical verses, physical acts, the text of the *haggadah*, and the manner of its enunciation are all part of one event, with each illuminating the other. *Notes on Akiba*, as theatre, participates in these mutually interpretive relations and contributes its own interpretations, both to the performance of the Seder and to the text of the *haggadah*. Note also that Kushner and Mayer declare that they are about to *perform* an exegesis. They present interpretation itself as performance. We will return to this later on.

Even beyond the Seder, Jewish societies cultivated exegesis not just as an intellectual endeavor but also as a religious observance in and of itself. It is part of the religious commandment known as *talmud torah*, or Torah Study, the commandment to learn and interpret religious texts. Torah Study is an obligating practice in Jewish religion, and will be central for the rest of my discussion in this book. It therefore merits some elaboration.

The ideal of Torah Study as a prestigious religious act was fully articulated by the Rabbis in Late Antiquity. The Rabbis perceived a fundamental breach between their time and the biblical past they interpreted, especially with regard to the possibility of access to the divine. The rabbinic historical consciousness contrasted the times of the Hebrew Bible, when there was a possibility of directly knowing God's will via divine revelation or prophecy, with the Rabbis' own period, when these routes all-in-all ceased to serve as viable options. The Hebrew Bible was now considered a sealed canon that cannot be further expanded, and the only path of approaching God's demands and understanding them is through human interpretations of the text given by him, the Torah. Importantly, the Rabbis did present a sense of continuity between their own moment and the original giving of the Torah at Mount Sinai. While this mythical event cannot of course be historically verified, Jewish tradition usually dates it around the fourteenth century BCE – that is, many centuries before the Rabbis. Nevertheless, the Rabbis asserted that their interpretations, however novel they might seem, were in fact also given at Sinai. Such a statement, however, already operates within a framework in which the Rabbis define themselves vis-à-vis a sealed canon, with the very act of sealing serving as a temporal borderline between past and present.

This sealed canon, as Moshe Halbertal claims, did not become the source of unified, monolithic truth – but quite the opposite. It served as a stimulus to a plethora of possible interpretations, since almost all meanings had to be derived from within it. The rabbinic exegetical practice known as *midrash* often extracts from the biblical text multiple meanings that go far beyond the text's literality, at times even against it, and that also greatly differ from one another. Furthermore, once the canon was sealed, Halbertal maintains, 'authority was removed from the writers of the text and transferred to its interpreters; denied to the prophets and awarded to the Sages' (p. 19). Not all Jewish religious cultures, both contemporaneous and subsequent, fully ascribed to this rabbinic historiographical narrative, and some continued to make claims of direct access to the divine. Nevertheless, this narrative had a formative impact on the idea and practice of Torah Study, which became a religious obligation in its own right, and arguably the most prestigious of religious practices. It was considered the ultimate mode of engaging with God's words. Gradually, the concept of Torah Study was expanded beyond the biblical text also to include the study of its rabbinic interpretations that were consequently also interpreted time and again.

Joshua Levinson (2004) describes the rabbinic consciousness as dialogic, in the sense that the Rabbis, as interpreters, placed themselves 'both inside and outside the text at the same time' (p. 524). Levinson analyzes a genre of rabbinic writing he calls 'the exegetical narrative'. It is a technique of interpreting a biblical story by combining overt exegesis, which cites and interprets specific biblical verses, with a narrative that retells the story in creative ways. In Levinson's words, it is 'composed of a story which simultaneously *represents* and *interprets* its biblical counterpart' (p. 498, my emphasis). Since the exegetical narrative juxtaposes biblical citations, exegetical comments, and innovative storytelling, it explicitly distinguishes 'between the old and the new, between the verse and its rewriting' (p. 500) and puts the tension between them into display. In other words, rabbinic dialogism maintains a double temporality, between past and present, and highlights this duality through the interplay between representation and interpretation. As we will see later on, this will have much consequence in understanding theatrical exegeses and their own negotiations of past traditions and the present time of performance.

As an obligatory religious practice, Torah Study also has bodily dimensions. It is a type of performance, even if not always explicitly acknowledged as such. Traditional Torah Study in the *beit-midrash* seldom entails reading in silent solitude, but rather in audible enunciation. A common studying practice is called *havruta* (Aramaic for 'friendship'), whereby the text is read aloud with a partner and then discussed and analyzed through vocal conversation. That is to say, the traditional mode of Torah Study is embodied dialogue. Furthermore, in different communities, Torah Study acquired its own performative nonverbal traditions as to how to practice it, such as a specific musicality for pronouncing the text, or particular body movements that accompany the study.

Textual interpretation is rooted so deep in Jewish religious practice that it resurfaces also in unexpected places. The earliest extant Hebrew play, Leone de' Sommi's aforementioned *A Comedy of Betrothal*, is such a case. On the surface, it is a typical Renaissance comedy about love, sex, and money – largely unconcerned with matters of religion.

The main plot of the play follows the love of the young Beruriah and her betrothed, Yedidiah. When Yedidiah's father, Shalom, dies in another city, and according to rumor bequeaths nothing to him, Beruriah's parents are quick to engage their daughter with another man. In his plight, Yedidiah goes to the corrupt rabbi Rav Hamdan (a name that can be translated as Rabbi Greedy), who devises a plan to manipulate *halacha*, or Jewish religious law, in order to compel Beruriah's parents to wed her with Yedidiah. This includes Yedidiah sleeping with Beruriah before she gets married, and then twisting several *halachic* arguments around so that neither of them will be punished for it. Such circumstances would leave her parents no choice but to consent to their marriage. Things, however, do not go as planned: the couple gets caught mid-act and Yedidiah is accused of sexual assault. In the worst possible timing, his father's former slave, Shoval, arrives in town and reveals that he is the one who got all the inheritance. Only then does Yedidiah learn that his father had died. In his distress, Yedidiah pleads guilty to all charges and is about to get thrown in jail. Only the intervention of another Rabbi, Rabbi Amitai (which can roughly be translated as Rabbi Truthful), saves him. The Rabbi examines the father's will and notes that it stipulates that indeed all of his possessions are to be given to Shoval, except one piece of property that Yedidiah may choose. Rabbi Amitai advises that Yedidiah will choose the slave himself. A Talmudic dictum stating that whatever a slave acquires automatically belongs to his master will allow Yedidiah to gain ownership over his father's entire fortune.

Rabbi Amitai claims that this was the father's intention all along. Yedidiah does so and, being rich again, gets the permission of Beruriah's parents to marry her.

A Comedy of Betrothal utilizes the potential of textual interpretation as a comic device, both malevolent and benevolent. Rabbi Amitai demonstrates the scope and inventiveness made possible by close interpretation of a text, the father's will, for the sake of his student's salvation and love's triumph (although modern readers, attuned to class inequity, might find this solution troubling). Rav Hamdan, on the other hand, exemplifies the dangerous aspects of this very same interpretive practice. One of the characters in the play disparagingly describes Rav Hamdan as a trickster-interpreter of Scripture, one who 'shows seventy sides in the Torah' (p. 88). Strikingly, the idea that the Torah has seventy sides, or 'faces' (*panim*), appears in Jewish sources since the Middle Ages as a positive trait, expressing the variety and plurality of possible legitimate interpretations that may be extracted from it. It is a central justification and rationale of Torah Study. Here, Rav Hamdan abuses the very same characteristic. Throughout the play, Rav Hamdan is actively manipulating *halacha* in order to promote lasciviousness, greed, and immorality, thus unveiling the interpretive system's own fluidity and elasticity, the fact that it does not necessarily maintain any stable moral core. It is a dark, uneasy portrayal of Jewish tradition's most prestigious religious practice.

De' Sommi's play is hardly an attack on the practice of textual interpretation and the religious establishment that promotes it. After all, Rabbi Amitai uses the very same practice to save Yedidiah. Rather, the play amounts to a comic interrogation of the many facets of textual interpretation. Yet there is also a sense of loss, perhaps even of mourning, that underlies this comedy. Showing the divine law as entirely open to interpretation, including by scoundrels such as Rav Hamdan, reveals its lack of inherent meaning and the inaccessibility of its source. Indeed, it is perhaps fitting that the interpreted document by the play's end is a dead father's will – the words of which are only left for us to interpret this way or that. It is perhaps not incidental that this dead father's name, Shalom, is, according to several rabbinic sources, also one of God's names. There are parallels between the two Rabbis' interpretive techniques – the one of God's law; the other of the father's will – in the sense that both are marked, indeed enabled, by the author's absence. This does not mean that the play implies that 'God is dead' in some secularist way. Rather, it is an expression of the loss and distance experienced by a religious community. At the same time, it conveys the ways in which this community acknowledges and addresses loss by undertaking the task of interpretation. In this sense, the play captures and dramatizes the sense of temporal rupture, and perhaps even crisis, that textual interpretation as religious practice harbors.

This sense of temporal rupture is significant for our discussion because, as mentioned earlier, time is of paramount importance both for the debates surrounding religion and secularization and for the theatre. If the secularization thesis assumes a linear progression of time, that leaves religion in the past, it is noteworthy that some religious traditions – such as the rabbinic one – in fact also emerged out of a sense of discontinuity with the past. Ironically, one thing we may share with the past is its consciousness of rupture from its *own* past. Torah Study is a performative practice that negotiates this temporal rupture. What happens, then, when its negotiations of the past are combined with theatre's negotiations of the past?

Up until recently (and still so in some Orthodox communities), Torah Study was exclusively a male domain, and consequently espoused male-dominated interpretations. However, several contemporary women theatre artists have incorporated practices of Torah Study into their performances in order to promote alternative engagements with religious canonical texts. The Theatre Company Jerusalem (TCJ) is a theatre group active in Jerusalem since the early 1980s that developed an experimental theatrical language to convey feminist interpretations to Jewish religious texts. In the 2009 Hebrew book *Secret Stage of Midrash*, Aliza Elion Israeli, the group's playwright, describes their goal to fashion an 'actress-homilist [...] that more than telling the story, provides exegesis to it' (p. 96). Elion Israeli's differentiation between storytelling and exegesis recalls the tension Levinson found between representation and interpretation in the rabbinic exegetical narrative, but also her understanding, like Kushner's, that exegesis is also performance. In some of TCJ's pieces, such as *Sarah – Take 2* (Jerusalem, 1994), the interplay between representation and interpretation, between enactment and exegesis, was built into the theatrical event. The performance was pre-ceded by a session of *havruta* studies, in which the audience learned and interpreted together the rabbinic texts that served as basis to the show they were about to watch – in this case, about the biblical figure of Sarah (pp. 141–42). This is one strategy of maintaining a productive dialogue between representation (the enactment *of* Sarah) and inter-pretation (studying *about* her), while also foregrounding the distinction between the two. In this sense, as the group simultaneously juxtaposes the biblical myth with their con-temporary interpretations of it and distinguishes between them, TCJ follows rabbinic dialogic poetics. However, while the Rabbis of Late Antiquity set the theatre and the *beit-midrash* in rivalry, TCJ created an event that drew from both performative traditions.

In other cases, the performance of Torah Study is incor-porated into the fictional drama presented onstage. Israeli playwright Yosefa Even-Shoshan's *The Maiden of Ludmir* (Khan Theatre of Jerusalem, 1998) follows the remark-able historical figure of Hanna-Rachel Verbermacher (1805–1888), the only woman in Hasidic history to have become a religious leader, amidst much controversy. In one lengthy scene in the play, Hanna-Rachel gathers a group of women for a session of Torah Study. The women discuss at length a passage from the Babylonian Talmud (tractate *Berachot* 61a) that interprets verses from Genesis about the creation of Man and Woman, and specifically the creation of Eve from Adam's rib. The Talmudic discussion, through detailed exegesis of words and even letters in the biblical text, relates two competing models of creation: one that is clearly hierarchical and claims that the word 'rib' designates a lower part of the body, and another that points out that the Hebrew word for 'rib' (*tsela*) also means 'side'. This interpretation therefore postulates, somewhat like Aristophanes in Plato's *Symposium*, that the first person was an androgynous creature, with male and female bodies on each side. As the women studying this passage in the play conclude, this interpretation suggests equality between the genders rather than hierarchy (pp. 102–05).

This scene is far more detailed than can be addressed here, and the characters' discussion follows the Talmud's own stalling on the minutiae of the biblical text, a seemingly redundant letter in a word here, or a recurrence of the same word in different contexts there – all in order to extrapolate various meanings from it. It is remarkable that a playwright will dedicate much stage-time for such exegetical 'nondramatic' deliberations, but this decision seems to convey Even-Shoshan's perception that in Jewish religious culture, study *is* drama, an act of confrontation and grappling with earlier interpretations through the learner's present-time concerns. The implications of the studied passage for gender politics are clear, but Hanna-Rachel also comments on the gender politics of the very act of studying, and women's traditional exclusion from it. She remarks: 'it is written in the books we are forbidden to read' (p. 105). Clearly, the act of interpretation intertwines with its content. The exegeses that female learners of the Torah perform will probably be different from those performed by males. In both cases, the act of study cannot be disentangled from the bodies performing it.

The group's study, as often is the case in traditional Torah Study, is also temporally multilayered; they perform their own interpretations of the Talmud's interpretations of the Bible. The performance of study brings together in one moment various historical or mythical times: the time of Creation, rabbinic academies in Late Ancient Babylonia, and nineteenth century Poland. Each period interprets earlier periods and their interpretations of even earlier periods. As noted above, the whole ideal of Torah Study emerged from a sense of temporal rupture, a discontinuity between the biblical past and the interpretive present. The scene from *The Maiden of Ludmir* demonstrates how study enables the learner to enter an intertemporal dialogue. She engages with traditional, canonic texts, and commits herself to them, while at the same time acknowledging the temporal distance between interpreter and text. Thus, the learner-interpreter both maintains and traverses temporal distance. In addition, the performance of this scene in the theatre adds another temporal layer – that of late twentieth century Israel – with the bodies of the actors joining the conversation with their own present-day concerns and agendas.

By reperforming scenes of Torah Study and textual interpretation onstage, theatre investigates what is at stake in the performance of study. However, theatre more often offers its own venue of study in which, rather than studying *about* figures, stories, or texts, the performer embodies and enacts them. In these cases, we move from the performance of study to performance *as* study – and this kind of study, to which we now turn, may have radical implications.

Embodiment: Seizing Tradition from Within

This section examines three plays that differ from each other greatly in terms of style, content, language, and religious disposition, but all share a bodily re-enactment of the Hebrew Bible that for our purposes can be considered exegetical. The idea of performance as study suggests the performing body as the main vehicle through which the interpretation of religious traditions takes place. This can occur in various ways. The simplest perhaps is cases in which theatre illuminates bodily elements that are already present in religious texts, and explores new meanings within them.

Israeli playwright Hanoch Levin's *The Torments of Job* (the Cameri Theatre, Tel Aviv, 1981) can shed light on these dynamics. *The Torments of Job* is a bold adaptation of the biblical book of Job. In the first half of the play, Levin more or less follows the biblical plotline: the rich Job loses his property and his children, and is afflicted by boils – followed by the arrival of his three friends and the theological debates ensuing between them. While the biblical source, however, frames Job's suffering in a heavenly debate between God and Satan about Job's righteousness, in Levin's play God does not appear at all as a dramatic character. Consequently, the main question debated between the friends in the play is not that of God's justice, as in the Bible, but rather of God's very existence. While Job steadfastly refuses to admit that God exists, his friends try to persuade him otherwise. Once the friends are finally successful in their attempts and Job reembraces God, Levin makes a sharp turn away from the biblical narrative. The Emperor's soldiers enter the stage and announce his decree that he himself is now God, that no other God exists, and that anyone who believes in another God will have a spit shoved up his anus. Now the friends try to persuade Job to denounce God but being so absorbed in his newly found religious ecstasy, he refuses to do so. The soldiers indeed punish him as threatened and then sell him to a circus manager, who displays him as a spectacle, together with two clowns, a stripper, and a dwarf who sings lecherous songs while masturbating. The ludicrous performance goes on until Job dies, with beggars licking up his vomit. All the later events in the play of course have no roots in the biblical text.

When first performed in Israel, the play caused an uproar that even reached parliament, demonstrating how volatile the juxtaposition between the biblical text and the performing body can be. Indeed, Levin utilizes the book of Job to stage a viscerally painful human existence in a world arguably devoid of God, and to delve into the futility of religious faith. In order to do so, he puts Job through immense physical violence, even beyond what the biblical text dictates. Here, however, I wish to focus specifically on the first part of the play, where Job's bodily afflictions still follow the Bible, and briefly explore how Levin interprets them theatrically.

In the biblical account, after Job loses all of his possessions and his children, God grants Satan permission to hurt him physically in order to test whether Job is indeed a pious man, or will finally break and curse God. Satan inflicts Job with boils and Job takes 'a potsherd to scratch himself' as he sits in the ashes (Job 2:7–8). Levin, in his stage directions, elaborates on this moment, taking place immediately after the corpses of Job's dead children are brought in front of him. He depicts Job sitting across his children's bodies and beginning to itch, almost absentmindedly. The itch continues, becomes stronger and stronger, culminating with Job scratching frantically, tearing off his underwear, and remaining naked, screaming like a beast (p. 67). Levin does not only re-enact the itching from the biblical text but also develops it into a leitmotif later in the play. During the theological debates with his friends, one of them, Eliphaz, argues: 'You're steeped in your itching but you know / Under your skin that God exists' (p. 71). Later on, Job himself says:

> But what is the meaning except suffering?
> I itch and itch,
> Try to dig into suffering, find meaning in it.
> And I tell you: There is nothing
> In the depths of suffering – only suffering! (p. 73)

Job's scratching therefore receives an ongoing interpretation by the characters as an act of digging. This interpretation is implied first by Eliphaz's suggestion that God is under Job's skin, suggesting that the itch might reveal that hidden divine presence. Then, it is fully elaborated by Job's rebuttal that despite 'digging into suffering' he finds nothing underneath except more suffering. Such an interpretation demands imagining the text as performance and studying it theatrically, for it relies on the bodily resemblance between itching and digging. This resemblance does not immediately arise from the biblical words alone, and requires giving account to the bodily presence described by the text and turning it into a physical metaphor. It can also serve as an implicit stage direction for the actor to perform itching as digging – to explore the physical act from within. As such, this sequence amounts to an exegetical performance of physical itching, an exploration of the bodily act in the text and its performative, theological, and existential meanings.

Levin reads the book of Job in an antagonistic manner, turning it into a tale that decries any faith in divine order. At the same time, however, Levin joins a longer tradition of addressing fundamental theological questions through the study, interpretation, and retelling of religious canonical texts. Via theatre's unique utilization of the body onstage, Levin extricates corporeal elements from the biblical text and makes his claims through them. Physical gestures and pain are the lenses that theatre provides Levin in order to read the Bible and stage his argument against God.

Levin's elaboration on Job's itching clearly conveys his own concerns and occupations, and it is probably quite removed from the Bible's intentions, but it does take its cue from a bodily element that is present in its source. Levin may have given a completely new meaning to Job's suffering body, but the suffering body itself is already central to the biblical text. In other cases, however, the original text may suppress or downplay a physicality that resurfaces through theatrical performance. In these instances, the very presence of the performing body is in direct tension with the traditional reading of the text.

Such is the case with the solo performance *VaTahar VaTeled*, meaning 'And She Conceived; and She Gave Birth' in biblical Hebrew (Tmuna Theatre, Tel Aviv, 2014). In this performance, Rachel Keshet, an Israeli Orthodox actor, retells the biblical stories of the matriarchs, accompanied by monologues she has written, in order to tackle the challenges of being a theatre artist, a religious person, and a mother of six, and the contrasting demands and expectations associated with these roles. Dressed in a bright yellow gown, with her long hair tied to the ceiling above to limit her movement, Keshet tells the stories of Sarah, Rebecca, Rachel, and Leah from the Hebrew Bible as myths of motherhood she confronts, struggles with, and deconstructs. Importantly, Keshet speaks the original biblical text, in the third voice. Thus, she maintains a certain distance from the biblical figures even as she embodies them. This distance is also manifested in the movement between the biblical text and Keshet's own monologues, in modern Hebrew. This movement highlights the dual temporality of the performance, in which the modern performer both engages with and distances herself from the ancient religious text. We may discern again an echo of the dialogic quality of rabbinic exegetical narratives, with their fluctuation between verses from the past and the voices of contemporary interpreters.

In one remarkable sequence, Keshet narrates the list of births given by Leah in Genesis 29:32–35 and 30:17–21:

> Leah conceived and bore a son, and named him Reuben; for she declared, 'It means: "The Lord has seen my affliction"; it also means: "Now my husband will love me"'. She conceived again and bore a son, and declared, 'This is because the Lord heard that I was unloved and has given me this one also'; so she named him Simeon. Again she conceived and bore a son and declared, 'This time my husband will become attached to me, for I have borne him three sons'. Therefore he was named Levi. She conceived again and bore a son, and declared, 'This time I will praise the Lord'. Therefore she named him Judah. [...] God heeded Leah, and she conceived and bore him a fifth son. And Leah said, 'God has given me my reward for having given my maid to my husband'. So she named him Issachar. When Leah conceived again and bore Jacob a sixth son, Leah said, 'God has given me a choice gift; this time my husband will exalt me, for I have borne him six sons'. So she named him Zebulun. Last, she bore him a daughter, and named her Dinah.

Note the consecutive, almost list-like quality of this text, its repetition of the formula 'she conceived [...] and bore' that gave Keshet's performance its name. Through the sons' various names, Leah expresses her sense of achievement in bearing sons and her hopes that with each new child, her estranged husband Jacob will finally love her. Significantly, the name of the daughter, Dinah, lacks any explanation. In her performance, Keshet begins reciting this text triumphantly, echoing the sense of accomplishment that patriarchal societies bestow upon women bearing sons. However, as the text progresses, Keshet performs it as if she is giving birth again and again, crouching lower and lower on the ground, with the groans, shoves, and visible effort of the body running counter to the rhythm of the biblical text. After the birth of Judah, Keshet cuts to a monologue that repetitively lists the endless chores of modern motherhood, thus reminding the audience of the gap between the biblical myth and contemporary reality. She then cuts back to the births of Issachar and Zebulun, and performs them once again with a sense of triumph and pride, as if the realities of birth and motherhood have been forgotten, or suppressed by myth and social expectations. Only with the birth of Dinah does this buoyant tone fade away, not only to convey that in patriarchal society a girl's birth is less valuable but also as a foreshadowing of Dinah's later sexual assault by Shechem (Genesis 34). Keshet ends the scene disturbingly by moving around the stage, restricted by her hair, and calling out to Dinah as a worried mother seeking her lost daughter. A sense of danger is already looming. This is an interpretation of the biblical words 'named her Dinah', for in Hebrew the words for 'named her' (*vatiqra et shma*) can also be understood as 'called out her name'.

This scene makes clear what is at stake in embodying a canonical religious text. The female body holds a knowledge that the patriarchal text downplays or even denies. The dry textuality of the list of births does not acknowledge the physical experience of giving birth, and Keshet's performance seeks to retrieve this bodily knowledge into the text. This occurs on a very physical level. While one may silently read the text as a straightforward list, without pause, Keshet's bodily effort in pronouncing it through the pain of giving birth changes its rhythm, pace, and punctuation, and demands the audience to approach it anew. Embodiment here disrupts textuality and serves as its critique.

My third example for theatre as embodied study is Tony Kushner's epic play *Angels in America* (*Part One: Millennium Approaches*: Mark Taper Forum, Los Angeles, 1990; *Part Two: Perestroika*: Mark Taper Forum, Los Angeles, 1992). The play famously follows the interconnected lives of several gay men with AIDS and the people around them in 1980s New York, during the Reagan presidency. Among those is Prior Walter, who early on in the play reveals he is diagnosed HIV positive. During the play, Prior is encountered by a female angel that appoints him as the angels' prophet to humankind. For reasons that are too intricate to detail here, the angels demand that humankind stops moving and progressing, claiming that human mobility and capability for change drove God out of this world. The play follows Prior as he tries to cope with the prophecy he received from the Angel. Towards the end of *Angels in America*, Prior chooses to reject it. The Angel, clearly upset, visits him in his hospital bed, where Prior is accompanied by a Mormon woman named Hannah. Prior confronts the furious angel and asks for Hannah's assistance. He reminds her it was her idea to 'reject the vision' and that she claimed there was 'scriptural precedent for that'. When Prior asks Hannah what he's supposed to do, the distraught Hannah finally blurts out:

HANNAH: (*Overlap*) You... you... wrestle her.
PRIOR: SAY *WHAT*?
HANNAH: It's an angel, you... just... grab hold and say... oh what was it, wait, wait, umm... OH! Grab her, say 'I will not let thee go except thou bless me!' Then wrestle with her till she gives in.
PRIOR: YOU wrestle her, I don't know how to wrestle, I... (p. 250; original emphases)

Despite his protestation, Prior does finally enter the fray and wrestles the Angel, while following Hannah's directions, reciting the text 'I... will not let thee go except thou bless me' and then adding some of his own words. Prior's wrestling with the Angel goes on quite spectacularly for a while, until the Angel surrenders, complaining that she had torn a muscle in her thigh. Prior is not impressed, remarking that his leg has been 'burning for months' due to his illness (p. 251).

The 'scriptural precedent' that Prior and Hannah are referring to is Genesis 32:25–33. In these verses, Jacob is about to return home, to the Land of Canaan, after many years away. On the verge of reentering the land, he has a nighttime encounter with a mysterious man (who later interpretations identify as an angel). The two wrestle until the break of dawn and Jacob is injured at the thigh muscle during the struggle. At dawn, the man asks Jacob to let him go, to which Jacob replies: 'I will not let you go, unless you bless me.' As a blessing, the man changes Jacob's name to Israel and disappears, leaving Jacob limping due to his injury.

In the Bible, this scene serves as a foundational moment in which Jacob receives the name Israel, a name of subsequent national importance, but Kushner recruits it to the contemporary struggles of the LGBTQ community and of people with AIDS. Once again, theatre serves to highlight the biblical text's bodily dimensions. The Angel and Prior's references to their injured legs clearly allude to Jacob's limping at the end of the biblical encounter. By reading the biblical text through the body, especially through Prior's leg, Kushner ties it with current-day concerns about disease and the vulnerable body. Another bodily intervention Kushner conducts with regard to his biblical source is switching the Angel's gender from male to female. As I explored in detail elsewhere (2012), this further serves to queer the scene and align it with contemporary sexual politics.

Angels in America unfolds to reveal what Prior stands to gain personally and politically from wrestling with the Angel. Following this scene, Prior climbs a ladder to Heaven (another theatrical allusion to Jacob), where he meets with the angels' council. There, Prior demands and receives the angels' blessing, just as Jacob did. This blessing is what enables him to live on with HIV and steer the play towards its hopeful epilogue, in which he addresses the audience and declares that gay people and people with AIDS will not die secret deaths anymore and will become full citizens. This is a remarkable political and theological move when one bears in mind the reaction of many religious institutions to the AIDS epidemic at the time. Voices on the political and religious right in the USA, including persons close to the Reagan administration, declared the epidemic to be a divine punishment for the sin of homosexuality and an expression of the 'wrath of God'. In response, Kushner offers an alternative religious discourse. He employs the story of Jacob and the Angel in order to propose a counter-myth, based on a foundational religious text, which can stand up against the religious right's own use of the Bible. Importantly, the person acquainting Prior with the wrestling myth is a religious Mormon woman, Hannah. Later in the play, Prior meets in Heaven the dead Jewish grandmother of his ex-lover Louis, Sarah Ironson. She tells him in Yiddish that, 'You should struggle with the Almighty [...] It's the Jewish way' (p. 269). Even though Sarah calls wrestling with God 'the Jewish way', its inheritor is, significantly, a non-Jewish gay man with AIDS. Both Hannah and Sarah give voice to a *religious* legacy that does not call for pious obedience, but rather for confrontation with the divine. It advocates wrestling with God, instead of succumbing to his wrath. Kushner therefore crystalizes a politically potent theological paradigm that can be authorized by religious tradition, to counter the usage made of Scripture for legitimizing the right wing's political ethos.

It should be noted that Prior is entirely aware that he is re-enacting the myth, staging it a second time as it were. Hannah teaches Prior the verses he needs to speak, indeed to *cite*, as he performs the mythical struggle once again. The temporal dimension is important here: the myth about Jacob and the Angel is notably a 'scriptural precedent'. A precedent is anchored in the past yet has vital implications for the present – very much like religion itself. In other words, Prior's wrestling is an act of engaging with the religious past again, from the present's standpoint. For Prior, re-enacting the role of Jacob and wrestling with the Angel would require him to play an ultra-masculine role, from which he sarcastically distances himself ('YOU wrestle her, I don't know how to wrestle'). With this statement, Prior is taking over Jacob's role but in a way that permits a somewhat remote perspective on the physically violent masculinity encoded in the biblical story. Furthermore, by wrestling with the Angel, Prior chooses to reperform a religious tradition with his own body, a body of a gay man with AIDS that in many ways has been marginalized and ostracized in the name of this very tradition. This highlights Prior's decisive political repositioning in relation to the tradition he embodies. By being fully aware that he is reperforming a myth, Prior takes a more overt stance vis-à-vis the scriptural canon. The fact that Prior explicitly situates himself in relation to this canon turns its reperformance into a clearly self-conscious act, a choice to embody the canon while revising it. Like the rabbinic dialogic consciousness, Prior rejects prophecy and instead situates himself both inside and outside the religious text he re-enacts.

In a sense, Prior's wrestling scene can also serve as an image of theatrical performances of religious traditions in general. By being aware that he is reperforming the Jacob myth, Prior is like any actor who performs a religious text or practice. Like Prior, who temporarily takes upon himself the role of Jacob, the actor who plays Job in *The Torments of Job*, for example, also becomes Job just for a while. Like Prior, other actors also negotiate their otherness in relation to the religious tradition they embody. In fact, it is this sense of distance, or tension, between the performer and religious traditions that enables theatrical exegesis. Through it, the personal investments and the politics of the body inform and give meaning to any dialogic engagement with religion.

The body brings with it such elements as aching, desire, sexuality, vulnerability, or disease that offer new ways of engaging with religious traditions. This engagement can be confrontational or reverent, it can express faith, or the lack of it, it may stem from a 'religious' or 'secular' point of view, but in any case it demands the co-presence of the performing body, with its present-time concerns, and religious traditions. This co-presence is what enables performance to become a form of study. By temporarily embodying a religious text, and by situating oneself in relation to it, the performer in many ways seizes tradition from within. By becoming Jacob, Leah, or Job for a moment, the performer – be that Prior, Keshet, or Job's actor – does not necessarily identify with the biblical figure (though that might be the case), but rather works through religious traditions, simultaneously within and against them, and thus interrogates and studies their contemporary implications.

Prior's act of consciously entering the wrestling can be seen as akin to the proclamation 'and now we will perform an exegesis' in Kushner's *Notes on Akiba*. In both cases, there is a declared moment of entering engagement, a self-aware intervention with past traditions that also presents itself as such, shows itself to others, and maintains the duality and distance between performer and tradition. By providing this interplay between text and its embodied study, theatre allows for a unique mode of seizing tradition from within in order to play it out with a difference.

Exegesis at Play

While all of my examples up until now depicted theatrical interpretations of Jewish religious texts and rituals, my final case study involves a performance that applies a Jewish exegetical technique on a non-Jewish text from the Western dramatic canon. If until now I showed how theatre has unique modes of interpreting Jewish religious traditions, now I wish to switch the direction of inquiry and examine how Jewish religious traditions inform the very practice of theatrical interpretation. This will demonstrate the breadth of potential hybridity that the intersection of theatre and

Judaism enables. It can take place not only in drama's content but also within the mechanisms of theatre.

In 2013, a spoken word adaptation of *The Tragedy of Macbeth* premiered in Jerusalem, performed by a group of young actors called the Victor Jackson Show. Over the past decade, this group has been exploring the poetics of rap, hip-hop, and spoken word poetry, and their integration into theatrical performance. The group examines the performativity of language, especially as developed in these contemporary genres of urban poetry, and inquires how it can be returned to the theatre stage. In their adaptation of *Macbeth*, the group wed Shakespeare's performative language with that of contemporary spoken word poetry. They retranslated the play in order to stress, as stated in the show, 'the power of words'.

The power of words in *Macbeth* is manifest in several layers. First, it is present in the play's plot, through the power of a few words in the Weird Sisters' prophecy to trigger Macbeth into action. Secondly, the play's adaptation emphasizes the power of words in the history of its reception. The performance begins with reference to the superstition regarding the alleged curse accompanying the mention of the Scottish Play's name. At the same time, the show celebrates the theatrical performativity of language manifest both in Shakespeare's theatre, where words famously conjured the fictional world on a relatively empty stage, and in the contemporary poetics of spoken word performances. While the show explicitly alludes mainly to Shakespeare and spoken word as cases of performative language, another important, implicit intertext for the production's emphasis on words and their power is the Jewish mystical tradition regarding the creative force of Hebrew letters. This tradition becomes an interpretive and performative apparatus governing the show.

In the Hebrew Bible, God creates the world through speech. From the initial statement 'let there be light' (Genesis 1:3) on, words rather than physical acts have the performative power of conjuring reality. Due to the primary role of speech acts in the biblical account, later Jewish traditions also imagined the building blocks of Creation mainly in verbal and textual terms. One strand of this imagination depicts the world as created through the combination of Hebrew letters. The idea appears most famously and influentially in the Late Ancient cryptic treatise *Sefer Yetsirah* ('The Book of Creation'). In this account, which continues throughout later Jewish mystical literature and meditation techniques, each Hebrew letter has its own force. It is an ontological entity harboring unique energy, and it holds performative power. This is yet another aspect of textuality's prominence in Jewish religious traditions, and again it goes hand in hand with performativity.

The notion that Hebrew letters hold performative power has subsequently also been attached to a hermeneutic system, that probably developed separately at first, which granted interpretive meaning to each letter in the Hebrew alphabet as well as to letters' various amalgamations. The meaning of the letter derived at times from its graphic shape, at times from its numerical value, and at times from various words beginning with that letter. The appearance of a letter in a certain word would be used to interpret that word through another word beginning with the same letter. This latter variant will be of interest to us here.

A similar technique appears in the spoken word *Macbeth*, where Shakespeare's play has been translated and adapted so that various Hebrew words are deconstructed into letters in order to supposedly unearth their deeper meaning. This is conducted mainly by the three street Youths, who replace the Weird Sisters in this adaptation. In one scene, as they first meet Macbeth, the Youths engage in a jam session of sorts, interpreting the name Macbeth. The most common Hebrew spelling of 'Macbeth' is the sequence of letters *mem kuf bet tav*. Therefore, one of the Youths suggests:

> Macbeth –
> The *kuf* between the *mem* and the *bet*;
> A line (*kav*) separating wars (*milchamot*) and home (*bayit*).
> Do you get it?

In this interpretation, the second letter of Macbeth's name in Hebrew, *kuf*, designates a line, *kav*, which begins with the letter *kuf*. In the same manner, the first letter, *mem*, signifies wars (*milchamot*) and the third letter, *bet* – home (*bayit*). Thus, the first three letters in Macbeth's name create the sequence 'wars-line-home'. The line is supposed to separate wars from home, as Macbeth is leaving the battlefield behind on his journey to his castle and his wife. The Hebrew letters thus encapsulate the dramatic moment. The Youth seems to imply that this moment was already encoded in the letters of Macbeth's name, that he was indeed destined to go through this journey. The Youths continue with their wordplay:

YOUTH III: But the *mem* of Macbeth is not the *mem* of war (*milchama*) or of frightening (*metil mora*).
It is the *mem* of kingship (*melucha*).

YOUTH I: God save the king.

YOUTH III: He puts the *mem* in magnificent (*mefo'ar*),
Puts the *kuf* in crown (*keter*).

YOUTH I: But the spelling of *keter* is with a *kaf*.

YOUTH III: When Macbeth will be king that will be changed.

Here, the Youths use the Hebrew letters directly to promise Macbeth the throne. The ending quip, about Macbeth changing spelling in the future – since the word 'crown' in Hebrew is not spelled with a *kuf*, but with a different letter, *kaf* – can be seen in a twofold manner. On the one hand, it humorously exposes the recklessness of this kind of interpretation of fate via letters, and calls into question those who engage in such divination. On the other hand, predicting a future in which Macbeth controls spelling is ominous indeed. If words and letters *do* have performative power, having power over them is tantamount to omnipotence, as Macbeth grows to believe.

As a contemporary equivalent to the Witches, the Youths highlight the Jewish mystical underpinning of the performative usage of words. As street urchins of sorts, they combine it with the rhetoric and wordplay of urban spoken word genres, rap, and hip-hop. There is much irony, of course, in such a mystical interpretation of the Hebrew letters of a name which is not even originally Hebrew, and that in fact can be spelled in several different ways once translated. Nevertheless, Macbeth himself is taken by the Youths and continues to rely very heavily on words and their performative power. During the final confrontation between him and Macduff, when Macduff exclaims that he arrives without words, for they are limited and express far less than the sword, Macbeth retorts:

MACBETH: Idiot! Words are everything.

Look, Macduff:

Live! (*all dead characters around him spring back to life*)

Die! (*they die again*)

Darkness! (*all lights go out*)

Light! (*the lights return*)

Words are the essence.

Arriving here without words is like arriving with nothing.

Look around you!

A sword? A chair? This is a stick and that is a box.

They have become that only because we've said so.

I am invincible because words are eternal.

Words that said that none of woman born shall harm Macbeth.

Here Macbeth combines the performativity of language in the theatre with its mystical power over his own fate. In the theatre, the actor has the power to turn a stick into a sword and a box into a chair by simply saying so. Therefore, 'arriving here without words is like arriving with nothing' – with 'here' signifying the theatrical space itself. At the same time, the performative capacity of words in the theatre to conjure realities holds theological significance as well. Macbeth mimics the biblical God's ability to create the world with the words 'let there be light', as well as the divine capability of reviving the dead. Since, as a theatre actor, he can now control words and their ability to create a world, Macbeth believes he is omnipotent.

A moment later, however, in order to prove his point, Macbeth shoves Macduff's sword – the one that he declared a mere stick – into his own chest. He discovers to his horror that it has a real effect on him. Macduff famously reveals that he is indeed not of woman born, and the fatally wounded Macbeth replies: 'you have arrived without words you say'. He then coughs blood, says 'Blood. Macduff… a poet after all', and dies.

This would seem to suggest the precedence of reality over words. Macbeth was wrong in believing the words of the Youths. He was likewise wrong in believing that the sword became a sword merely by the words spoken in the theatre. This 'real' sword 'really' kills him. Yet of course, this is not entirely correct. On stage, Macbeth is killed by a stick, and it is noteworthy that he is required to utter the word 'blood' in order for blood to become theatrically present as the sign of his upcoming death. At least in the theatre, words do seem to create a world after all. Nevertheless, the power of words cannot be easily trusted. The final scene shows Macduff alone on stage when the three Youths enter, asking: 'Is it not Macduff? *Mem* to the *kuf* to the duff duff duff'. They begin deconstructing his name into letters as they did to Macbeth, implying that they might ensnare him in the very same net.

As far as the 'power of words' goes, the performance ends with an ambiguous tone indeed. On the one hand, words and Hebrew letters display a performative potency as a theatrical device drawn from Jewish mystical traditions. On the other hand, they prove seductive, deceptive, and fickle as a hermeneutic tool to interpret fate or reality. Thus, the show questions the performative force of language, and the value attached to it, at the same time as it asserts it and activates it.

Through intertextual links, whether consciously constructed or not, the Victor Jackson Show's *Macbeth* participates in a longer Jewish tradition of textual exegesis. Here, Shakespeare's *Macbeth* becomes Scripture, upon which a variety of traditional interpretive techniques are employed. The minutiae of *Macbeth*'s names, words, and images are interrogated and deconstructed for further meaning with the same meticulous attention to detail that Jewish exegetes gave the Hebrew Bible. What is striking here, for our current discussion, is the incorporation of a Jewish hermeneutic tradition into the very fabric of translating, interpreting, and performing Shakespeare's play. The notion that theatrical performance is an interpretation of a written play has justifiably been criticized in theatre studies of the past decades for putting performance in a subservient position in relation to text. Here, however, interpretation is a central component in the live theatrical event. Textual interpretation *is* performance, it is a game played between the Youths, and they enlist words and letters in order to display their interpretive virtuosity in public. This production utilizes text and textuality as part of its performative apparatus, and in doing so follows Jewish religious traditions in which textual interpretation is itself a performance. The employment of traditional Jewish hermeneutic techniques by the Victor Jackson Show demonstrates their performative quality, the ways in which they form a system of enacted strategies of study and interpretation that can be utilized in various contexts, even on non-Jewish texts.

That said, while evoking Jewish traditions regarding the performativity of Hebrew letters and their interpretation, this production hardly fully adheres to their religious or mystical underpinnings. As we have seen, the performance casts ironic doubt on the reliance on such beliefs. At the same time, the play does utilize these traditions to create a specifically Hebrew strategy through which Shakespeare is channeled and the theatrical power of words is celebrated. If mystical traditions imbue Hebrew letters with performativity, this *Macbeth* holds on to this performativity in order to reactivate it in the theatre, but divorces it from its mystical roots. The show engages with the performative potency of religious traditions without necessarily committing to their theological or metaphysical presuppositions. Rather than rejecting these suppositions, or fully embracing them, it would be more accurate to say that this show *plays* with them. Rather than 'religious' or 'secular', then, the stance this performance has towards the religious tradition it activates can best be described as playful.

Some might claim against this that a playful attitude towards religious traditions is necessarily a secular one. Playfulness is often understood as incompatible with religion, because the latter tends to be equated with sincerity. After all, religious people *truly believe* in what they do. Theatrical play, on the other hand, has a long history in the West of drawing suspicion as being insincere, as an art based on pretense. This stands at the core of the continuous phenomenon Jonas Barish influentially identified as the 'anti-theatrical prejudice'. It is with reconsidering theatrical playfulness and religion that I would like to conclude this book.

conclusion: playing with traditions in a post-secular age

I wish to argue that theatre's playfulness might actually be its most fruitful asset in current conversations about religion in the public sphere. The equation of religion and sincerity, on the other hand, might merit reassessment. In their joint study, *Ritual and Its Consequences* (2008), Adam B. Seligman, Robert P. Weller, Michael J. Puett, and Bennett Simon argue that the emphasis on sincerity in contemporary religious discourse stems from particular religious traditions, especially Protestantism, that have been applied to other religions. The religious act has come to be seen as one of self-expression that conveys the inner self of the person, her belief, or faith. However, the writers claim, in some religious traditions, the concept of play can prove more useful for understanding religious ritual. Ritual, like play, creates subjunctive, 'as if' conditions that offer an alternative experience of the world. This does not mean that play is not serious; it is very much so, in religion as in the theatre.

It does mean, however, that religion is not incompatible with play. A playful stance towards religious traditions therefore *can* be secularizing in some cases, but it can also be put in dialogue and on a continuum with some traditions' own activations of play.

Torah Study and exegesis are such activations, I argue. The performance of study, as we have seen, holds affinities with theatrical play in the sense that it creates a space where times intermingle through the performing body. It also exhibits dualities similar to those found in theatrical play. Theatre displays a simultaneous capability of being both inside and outside, of embodying a figure but not fully becoming it, of being both character and actor at the same live moment. Torah Study likewise allows the learner to commit herself to the religious material she interprets while at the same time remaining distinct from it, containing this duality within one body.

Why is this important? Because play, especially in the theatre, has the capacity to traverse binaries and dichotomies, and encompass things that otherwise seem to be opposites. In the theatre, bodies, objects, and spaces present themselves as if they are something else, while retaining their actual material presence. Theatre therefore has a propensity for upsetting binary definitions of identity, including those of 'religious' and 'secular'. Current conversations about religion often frame possible responses to it precisely as such a binary choice: one either fully conforms to religious decrees or wholeheartedly rejects them as a secular person. This dichotomy obscures the myriad and nuanced stances towards both religiosity and secularity, among individuals and communities. Theatrical play, I suggest, enables a shared inquiry into less dichotomous engagements with religion, as well as with secularity, especially in our post-secular age, when religion returns to the public sphere. Theatre enables us to play with religious traditions, and it can draw models for such play *from* religious traditions.

Instead of thinking of theatre in Jewish societies in terms of secularization, I have proposed in this book to consider it as a form of study – a notion that stems from Jewish religious traditions but also allows for maintaining distance and registering rupture. Theatre adds to Torah Study the dynamics of embodiment and enactment, and the interpretive dimensions enabled by them. Theatre-as-study serves as a site for constant bodily reconfigurations of one's relation to religious traditions.

Ali Pfefferman reciting the Torah on her living room coffee table, the actor playing Job, Rachel Keshet speaking the biblical verses about Leah, Prior re-enacting Jacob's struggle, and the Victor Jackson Show reactivating Jewish mystical traditions – all enter an engagement with religious figures, texts, and practices. Yet by doing so, they maintain a distance between themselves and the religious sources that they are performing, and encompass duality in one performing body. It is not so much a question whether the performers are 'religious' or 'secular', or anything in between. Rather, they enter this engagement as a conscious act of choice, and by bodily seizing tradition from within allow the audience to join them in interrogating religion's meanings for contemporary culture. The particular stance towards religion of course varies greatly from one performance to another, with some more antagonistic than others. That notwithstanding, theatre-as-study offers a playful practice of simultaneous commitment and noncommitment to religious traditions, for both performers and spectators. It enables activating these traditions but also deconstructing them, enacting them but not necessarily believing in them. I find such playful duality to be extremely valuable for the shared exploration in the theatre of religion's current reverberations in society's public sphere, in political debates, and within personal identities. Like Prior's angel, religious traditions are here to wrestle with, and theatre is a good place to play that out.

further reading

Martin Goodman's *A History of Judaism* offers a comprehensive survey of the complex development of Jewish religion. An excellent entry point to the topic of theatre in Jewish societies is Edna Nahshon's introductory essay for the anthology she edited, *Jewish Theatre: A Global View*, which usefully surveys the various attempts to define Jewish theatre, and outlines the inherent difficulties in such attempts. Nahshon's and Belkin's (2008) anthologies both display a comparative, global, and multifocal approach to the subject. Jacobs and Zeev Weiss allow for a rich understanding of rabbinic responses to Roman theatre. Kaufmann, Belkin (1997), and my own 2010 paper deal with Leone de' Sommi and the Jews of Renaissance Italy. Sandrow gives an eloquent survey of Yiddish theatre, complemented by the works of Berkowitz, Caplan, Nahshon (2016), and Veidlinger, among others. Abramson, Levy (1998), and Urian all deal with the place of Jewish religion in Israeli theatre and drama.

On the representation of Jewish ethnic identity on the stage, see Schiff, Erdman, and Bial (2005). Several of the studies below focus on the participation of Jews in modern theatrical cultures worldwide, such as in German theatre (Malkin and Rokem), Arab theatre (Moreh and Sadgrove), and American theatre (Bial, Erdman, Most, and the special issue of *TDR* dedicated to the subject, edited by Dolan and Wolf). Most's *Theatrical Liberalism* is of particular relevance for this book, as it addresses the ways in which religious traditions implicitly informed Jewish participation in American theatre. Bial's *Playing God* applies the concept of *midrash* to Broadway. Solomon offers a masterful study of *Fiddler on the Roof.*

Halbertal and Hartman Halbertal (1998) propose a theorization of the Jewish practice of *havruta* that also takes performance into account. For an illuminating ethnography of the traditional performance of Torah Study as social drama and play, see Heilman. On the mystical traditions regarding the performativity of Hebrew letters, see Tzahi Weiss.

Debates regarding the secularization thesis rage also in the scholarship of Jewish history. For both sides of the conversation see Feiner (who largely defends the thesis, at least in the context of European Jews, while citing theatre attendance among Jews in the eighteenth century as one of his prime evidences), and Joskowicz and Katz's edited volume, which provides good examples of studies that reevaluate the secularization theory in the Jewish context. For the implementation of post-secular sensitivities in theatre and performance studies, see Gharavi's introduction to

Religion, Theatre and Performance, and Chambers, du Toit, and Edelmen's introduction to *Performing Religion in Public*.

NOTE: Translations from the Hebrew Bible are from the New JPS Translation, with references to specific verse numbers following this translation's versification. All translations from the Palestinian Talmud, Avrom Goldfaden, Aliza Elion Israeli, and the Victor Jackson Show's *The Tragedy of Macbeth* are my own.

Abramson, Glenda. *Drama and Ideology in Modern Israel*. Cambridge: Cambridge University Press, 1998.

Asad, Talal. *Formations of the Secular: Christianity, Islam, Modernity*. Stanford: Stanford University Press, 2003.

―――. *Genealogies of Religion: Discipline and Reasons of Power in Christianity and Islam*. Baltimore: Johns Hopkins University Press, 1993.

Balme, Christopher B. *The Theatrical Public Sphere*. Cambridge: Cambridge University Press, 2014.

Barish, Jonas. *The Antitheatrical Prejudice*. Berkeley: University of California Press, 1981.

Batnitzky, Leora. *How Judaism Became a Religion: An Introduction to Modern Jewish Thought*. Princeton: Princeton University Press, 2011.

Belkin, Ahuva, ed. *Jewish Theatre: Tradition in Transition and Intercultural Vistas*. Tel Aviv: Tel Aviv University Press, 2008.

―――, ed. *Leone de' Sommi and the Performing Arts*. Tel Aviv: Tel Aviv University Press, 1997.

Berger, Peter L., ed. *The Desecularization of the World: Resurgent Religion and World Politics*. Washington, DC: Ethics and Public Policy Center, 1999.

Berkowitz, Joel. *Shakespeare on the American Yiddish Stage*. Iowa City: University of Iowa Press, 2002.

―――, ed. *Yiddish Theatre: New Approaches*, Oxford: Littman Library of Jewish Civilization, 2003.

Berkowitz, Joel and Barbara Henry, eds. *Inventing the Modern Yiddish Stage: Essays in Drama, Performance, and Show Business*. Detroit: Wayne State University Press, 2012.

'Best New Girl.' *Transparent*, season 1, episode 8, written by Bridget Bedard, directed by Jill Soloway, Amazon, 26 Sep. 2014.

Bial, Henry. *Acting Jewish: Negotiating Ethnicity on the American Stage and Screen*. Ann Arbor: University of Michigan Press, 2005.

———. *Playing God: The Bible on the Broadway Stage*. University of Michigan Press, 2015.

Bruce, Steve. *Secularization: In Defence of an Unfashionable Theory*. Oxford: Oxford University Press, 2011.

Buber, Martin. 'Reach for the World, Ha-Bima!' (1929). *Martin Buber and the Theater*. Ed. Maurice Friedman. New York: Funk and Wagnalls, 1969. 88–91.

Caplan, Debra. *Yiddish Empire: The Vilna Troupe, Jewish Theater, and the Art of Itinerancy*. Ann Arbor: University of Michigan Press, 2018.

Casanova, José. *Public Religions in the Modern World*. Chicago: University of Chicago Press, 1994.

Chambers, Claire Maria, Simon W. du Toit, and Joshua Edelmen. 'Introduction: The Public Problem of Religious Doings.' *Performing Religion in Public*. Eds. Claire Maria Chambers, Simon W. du Toit, and Joshua Edelmen. Basingstoke: Palgrave Macmillan, 2013. 1–24.

Chambers, E.K. *The Mediaeval Stage*. Oxford: Clarendon Press, 1903.

Davis, Tracy C. 'Performative Time.' *Representing the Past: Essays in Performance Historiography*. Eds. Charlotte M. Canning and Thomas Postlewait. Iowa City: University of Iowa Press, 2010. 142–67.

Dolan, Jill, and Stacy Wolf, eds. *Jewish American Performance*. Special issue of *TDR* 55:3 (2011).

Dymov, Osip. *Bronx Express*. In *God, Man, and Devil: Yiddish Plays in Translation*. Trans. and ed. Nahma Sandrow. Syracuse: Syracuse University Press, 1999. 261–305.

Elion Israeli, Aliza. *Secret Stage of Midrash: Theatre Company Jerusalem*. Tel-Aviv: Yediot Aharonot, 2009 [Hebrew].

Erdman, Harley. *Staging the Jew: The Performance of an American Ethnicity, 1860–1920*. New Brunswick, NJ: Rutgers University Press, 1997.

Even-Shoshan, Yosefa. *The Maiden of Ludmir: A Story of a Woman Who Asked for a Man's Soul*. Trans. Elisheva Greenbaum and Avraham Leader. In *Wanderers and Other Israeli Plays*. Ed. Sharon Aronson-Lehavi. London, New York and Calcutta: Seagull Books, 2009. 71–124.

Feiner, Shmuel. *The Origins of Jewish Secularization in Eighteenth-Century Europe*. Trans. Chaya Naor. Philadelphia: University of Pennsylvania Press, 2011.

Gharavi, Lance, ed. *Religion, Theatre and Performance: Acts of Faith*. London: Routledge, 2012.

Goldfaden, Avrom. 'The Music of my Musical Plays' (1889). *Selected Writings*. Ed. Shmuel Rozhansky. Buenos Aires: YIVO, 1963. 255–61 [Yiddish].

Goodman, Martin. *A History of Judaism*. London: Penguin Books, 2017.

Habermas, Jürgen. 'Notes on Post-Secular Society.' *New Perspectives Quarterly* 25:4 (2008): 17–29.

———. 'Religion in the Public Sphere.' *European Journal of Philosophy* 14:1 (2006): 1–25.

Halbertal, Moshe. *People of the Book: Canon, Meaning and Authority*. Cambridge, MA: Harvard University Press, 1997.

Halbertal, Moshe and Tova Hartman Halbertal. 'The Yeshiva.' *Philosophers on Education: Historical Perspectives*. Ed. Amélie Oksenberg Rorty. London: Routledge, 1998. 458–69.

Harrison, Jane Ellen. *Themis: A Study of the Social Origins of Greek Religion, with an Excursus on the Ritual Forms Preserved in Greek Tragedy by Professor Gilbert Murray and a Chapter on the Origin of the Olympic Games by Mr. F.M. Cornford*. Cambridge: Cambridge University Press, 1912.

Heilman, Samuel C. *The People of the Book: Drama, Fellowship and Religion*. Chicago: University of Chicago Press, 1983.

Jacobs, Martin. 'Theatres and Performances as Reflected in the Talmud Yerushalmi.' *The Talmud Yerushalmi and Graeco-Roman Culture*, Vol. I. Ed. Peter Schäfer. Tübingen: Mohr Siebeck, 1998. 327–47.

Jakobsen, Janet R., and Ann Pellegrini. 'Introduction: Times Like These.' *Secularisms*. Eds. Janet R. Jakobsen and Ann Pellegrini. Durham, NC: Duke University Press, 2008. 1–35.

Joskowicz, Ari, and Ethan B. Katz, eds. *Secularism in Question: Jews and Judaism in Modern Times*. Philadelphia: University of Pennsylvania Press, 2015.

Kaufmann, David. 'Leone de Sommi Portaleone (1527–92), Dramatist and a Founder of a Synagogue at Mantua.' *JQR* 10:3 (1898): 445–61.

Kushner, Tony. *Angels in America: A Gay Fantasia on National Themes.* New York: Theatre Communications Group, 2003.

———. *Notes on Akiba.* In *Death and Taxes: Hydriotaphia & Other Plays.* New York: Theatre Communications Group, 2000.

Levin, Hanoch. *The Torments of Job.* In *The Labor of Life: Selected Plays.* Trans. Barbara Harshav. Stanford: Stanford University Press, 2003. 51–91.

Levinson, Joshua. 'Dialogical Reading in the Rabbinic Exegetical Narrative.' *Poetics Today* 25:3 (2004): 497–528.

Levy, Shimon. *The Bible as Theatre.* Brighton: Sussex Academic Press, 2002.

———. '"The Dybbuk" Revisited: Images of Religious Jews on the Israeli Stage.' *Israel Affairs* 4:3–4 (1998): 218–29.

———, ed. *Theatre and Holy Script.* Brighton: Sussex Academic Press, 1999.

Lipshitz, Yair. 'Performance as Profanation: Holy Tongue and Comic Stage in *Tsahut bedihuta deqiddushin*.' *Renaissance Drama* 36–37 (2010): 125–56.

———. 'The Jacob Cycle in *Angels in America*: Re-Performing Scripture Queerly.' *Prooftexts* 32:2 (2012): 208–38.

Malkin, Jeanette R., and Freddie Rokem, eds. *Jews and the Making of Modern German Theatre.* Iowa City: University of Iowa Press, 2010.

Moreh, Shmuel and Philip Sadgrove. *Jewish Contributions to Nineteenth-Century Arabic Theatre: Plays from Algeria and Syria.* Oxford: Oxford University Press, 1996.

Most, Andrea. *Making Americans: Jews and the Broadway Musical.* Cambridge, MA: Harvard University Press, 2005.

———. *Theatrical Liberalism: Jews and Popular Entertainment in America.* New York: New York University Press, 2013.

Nahshon, Edna, ed. *Jewish Theatre: A Global View.* Leiden: Brill, 2009.

———, ed. *New York's Yiddish Theater: From the Bowery to Broadway.* New York: Columbia University Press, 2016.

Postlewait, Thomas. 'The Sacred and the Secular: Reflections on the Writing of Renaissance Theatre History.' *Assaph: Studies in the Theatre* 12 (1996): 1–31.

Rozik, Eli. *Jewish Drama & Theatre: From Rabbinical Intolerance to Secular Liberalism.* Eastbourne: Sussex Academic Press, 2013.

Sandrow, Nahma. *Vagabond Stars: A World History of Yiddish Theater*. New York: Harper & Row, 1977.

Schiff, Ellen. *From Stereotype to Metaphor: The Jew in Contemporary Drama*. Albany: SUNY Press, 1982.

Schneider, Rebecca. *Theatre & History*. Basingstoke: Palgrave Macmillan, 2014.

Seligman, Adam B., Robert P. Weller, Michael J. Puett, and Bennett Simon. *Ritual and Its Consequences: An Essay on the Limits of Sincerity*. Oxford: Oxford University Press, 2008.

Shoham, Hizky. 'Rethinking Tradition: From Ontological Reality to Assigned Temporal Meaning.' *European Journal of Sociology* 52:2 (2011): 313–40.

Smith, Jonathan Z. 'Religion, Religions, Religious.' *Critical Terms for Religious Studies*. Ed. Mark C. Taylor. Chicago: University of Chicago Press, 1998. 269–84.

Solomon, Alisa. *Wonder of Wonders: A Cultural History of Fiddler on the Roof*. New York: Picador, 2013.

Sommo, Yehudah (Leone de' Sommi). *Tsahut bedihuta deqiddushin (A Comedy of Betrothal)*. Ed. Hayyim Schirmann. Jerusalem: Tarshish and Dvir, 1965 [Hebrew].

Stark, Rodney. 'Secularization, R.I.P.' *Sociology of Religion* 60:3 (1999): 249–73.

Stein, Joseph, Jerry Bock, and Sheldon Harnick. *Fiddler on the Roof*. New York: Limelight Editions (reprint edition), 2004.

Taylor, Charles. *A Secular Age*. Cambridge, MA: Harvard University Press, 2007.

'The Symbolic Exemplar.' *Transparent*, season 1, episode 7, written by Faith Soloway, directed by Jill Soloway, Amazon, 26 Sep. 2014.

The Tragedy of Macbeth. Translated and adapted by Amit Ulman, together with Omer Havron, Iftach Leibovic, Dani Shapiro and Dana Yadlin. Directed by Amit Ulman. The Victor Jackson Show. The Incubator Theatre, Jerusalem, 14 Nov. 2013.

Tylor, Edward Burnett. *Primitive Culture: Researches into the Development of Mythology, Philosophy, Religion, Art, and Custom*. London: John Murray, 1871.

Urian, Dan. *The Judaic Nature of Israeli Theatre: A Search for Identity*. Trans. Naomi Paz. Amsterdam: Harwood Academic Publishers, 2000.

VaTahar VaTeled ('And She Conceived; and She Gave Birth'). By Rachel Keshet and Hanna Vazana Grunwald. Tmuna Theatre, Tel Aviv. 21 Oct. 2014.

Veidlinger, Jeffrey. *The Moscow State Yiddish Theater: Jewish Culture on the Soviet Stage*. Bloomington: Indiana University Press, 2000.

Weiss, Tzahi. *Sefer Yeṣirah and Its Contexts: Other Jewish Voices*. Philadelphia: University of Pennsylvania Press, 2018.

Weiss, Zeev. *Public Spectacles in Roman and Late Antique Palestine*. Cambridge, MA: Harvard University Press, 2014.

Wilson, Bryan R. 'Aspects of Secularization in the West.' *Japanese Journal of Religious Studies* 3:4 (1976): 259–76.

acknowledgments

It is appropriate for a book about theatre and Judaism to begin with gratitude to the matchmaker. I am thankful to Freddie Rokem for making the connection between the editors of the *Theatre &* series, Jen Harvie and Dan Rebellato, and me, thus enabling this book's birth.

Jen Harvie and the anonymous readers of the manuscript offered generous and thorough critical observations that enabled me to articulate my argument and clarify my voice.

Through different stages of work on the book, Nicola Cattini, Sonya Barker, and Chloë Meyronnet from Red Globe Press (formerly Palgrave) supported the process with kindness and productive dialogue.

I thank Amit Ulman and the Victor Jackson Show for granting me permission to quote from their adaptation of *Macbeth*.

Mira Balberg, Hizky Shoham, and Moulie Vidas read earlier versions of the book and profoundly contributed to it with their thoughtful insights, comments, friendship, and encouragement.

My partner, Brachi Lipshitz, went through several phases of this book's various incarnations, and offered sharp, perceptive, and astute observations – always understanding before me where I wish to go and challenging me to take another step further. I am thankful to her, as always, with much love and admiration.

index

9 781352 005660